A Workbook *for* New Testament Greek

Grammar and Exegesis in First John

MARVIN R. WILSON

CHRIS ALEX VLACHOS

HENDRICKSON PUBLISHERS

To the New Testament Greek students
at Gordon College,
Wenham, Massachusetts,
and the Utah Institute for Biblical Studies,
Salt Lake City, Utah

A Workbook for New Testament Greek: Grammar and Exegesis in First John
© 1998 by Hendrickson Publishers, Inc.
P. O. Box 3473
Peabody, Massachusetts 01961-3473
All rights reserved
Printed in the United States of America

ISBN 978-1-56563-340-7

Third Printing — September 2008

This book is a thorough revision, updating, and expansion of *A Guide for the Study of the First Letter of John in the Greek New Testament,* by Marvin R. Wilson, © 1979 Baker Book House. Assigned 1985 to Marvin R. Wilson. Assigned 1997 to Hendrickson Publishers, Inc.

A Workbook *for* New Testament Greek

CONTENTS

PREFACE

Most first-year Greek students seem to be motivated by the same interest: they want to read the Greek New Testament as soon as possible. In the mind of beginning students, however, the drudgery of basic memory work—vocabulary, declensions, conjugations—seems to wear on unendingly. Accordingly, these potential Greek enthusiasts often feel their grammars have become little more than tedious tools for pedantically plowing through paradigms. They are chafing at the bit, anxious to see the historical and personal relevancy of all these exercises. They want to apply their newly acquired grammatical skills to the literary documents themselves. All too often, however, they have little systematic exposure to the biblical Greek text before completing their introductory grammar.

This workbook to 1 John has been produced to resolve this frustrating scenario. The present edition is designed for the student who is slightly past the midpoint in an introductory grammar and wishes to begin and complete the translation of a New Testament book.

First John is ideally suited for introducing students to the Greek text of the New Testament. First, the letter is short. Its five chapters of 105 verses can be studied in a limited amount of class time. The assignments that follow are conveniently broken down to an average of four verses each. Secondly, it gives a greater sense of accomplishment when an entire book is read rather than only sections of books.

Thirdly, the vocabulary and syntax of 1 John are about the simplest Greek for first-year students to master. Complex sentences and *hapax legomena* (words occurring but once) are relatively rare. The entire book of 1 John uses a vocabulary of only 234 Greek words, and (as you may see by browsing through the GREEK-ENGLISH DICTIONARY OF FIRST JOHN) many of these are common terms given in most introductory Greek grammars. In light of this, students who begin to work through 1 John soon come to realize that it is indeed possible to read biblical Greek. The resulting sense of accomplishment usually provides a needed encouragement for the beginner to continue the study of Greek on a more advanced level.

The assignments assume the student has already progressed through lesson 15 of Machen's grammar, lesson 28 of Wenham's grammar, or chapter 23 of Mounce's grammar and thus will already know words given in the earlier chapters of these grammars (e.g., ἀδελφός, ἀγάπη, κόσμος, υἱός, etc.). A knowledge of the conjugations and declensions given in the early chapters of the elementary grammars will also be assumed. Students will be encouraged when they see so many terms and forms that they already know.

The twenty-five assignments from 1 John are based on the Greek text shared by the twenty-seventh revised edition of the *Novum Testamentum Graece* and the fourth revised edition of the United Bible Societies' *Greek New Testament*. A VOCABULARY section at the beginning of each lesson provides definitions and parses forms that may as yet be unfamiliar to the student of elementary Greek. Various QUESTIONS listed under each assignment draw the student into the Greek text of 1 John. Space is provided so that answers and comments may be written in. Many of these questions review basic grammar.

Further questions given under the heading FOR FURTHER STUDY, however, aim at a more comprehensive understanding of Greek grammar and expose the student to various principles of exegesis and syntactical analysis. Most questions are followed by page numbers from selected volumes where answers may be discovered. These study exercises are not intended to exhaust the meaning of the text; rather, they are meant to acquaint the student with certain research procedures. In addition, they are designed to introduce the student to major bibliographic tools and resources for exegesis in the Greek New Testament. These include grammars, wordbooks, lexicons, dictionaries, concordances, and commentaries. All references employed in the study assignments are included in the bibliography.

Most of the questions in the FOR FURTHER STUDY section require more time and thought to answer. They provide students with the opportunity to explore the text more deeply and are especially suitable for classroom discussion. These include questions on etymology, textual criticism, and grammatical issues that may require a significant amount of time to research and answer. Biblical exegesis, however, must always move from seeking to understand what the text says (our primary focus in the VOCABULARY and QUESTIONS sections of the 25 assignments) to what the text teaches about God and God's relationship to the world. The FOR FURTHER STUDY questions, therefore, are most often based on a particular Greek word or clause of theological importance and are primarily aimed at uncovering theological and applicational aspects of the biblical segment being studied. Accordingly, sound exegesis is a process that starts with the biblical text and leads the exegete into discovering what relevance that text may have for today's church.

Expanding on the above, the broad process of biblical interpretation involves several steps. It starts with grammatical-historical exegesis, an examination of the words of the text in their original setting. This step is the very foundation of all biblical interpretation and is therefore the primary purpose and emphasis of this study guide. Utilizing the original language(s) of Scripture, students must learn how to find the verbal meaning of the text (what the author intended to say) within its historical, cultural, and literary context.

The second step is theological exegesis. Every biblical text is animated by some theological concern. This step seeks to determine the authoritative theological teaching or timeless theological principles within the passage. The final step involves the affective dimension of exegesis whereby the text is applied in concrete ways in the life of the contemporary Christian community. The FOR FURTHER STUDY questions usually focus more on either or both of the last two steps of exegesis than the first step mentioned above. Thus, many of the questions tend to be more complex and discussion-oriented. The QUESTIONS section of each assignment tends to focus on specific answers related to grammar, syntax, and word studies. But, by contrast, the FOR FURTHER STUDY section typically has wider-ranging questions that require broader knowledge of Scripture and theology. They require not so much a set, very precise answer as a theological discussion that will depend on the particular passage and on the viewpoints of students and teacher. In short, many of the questions require a certain level of grounding in theological thought and are intended to provoke a more sophisticated level of reflection upon the biblical text.

In a classroom setting, students are encouraged to prepare each assignment in advance of class. The teacher is urged to help by placing on the reserve shelf of the library all the research tools needed to complete the assignments in the *Workbook*. Since some libraries may not have all the reference works used in this guide, in many cases more than one reference is cited for a particular question. In the event that the students' work load is heavy, instructors can assign a limited number of QUESTIONS or divide them up among the students. Questions in the FOR FURTHER STUDY section can be made optional (for extra credit), or the student can be asked to choose one or more to answer. Results of the students' research can be shared when the passage is translated and discussed in class.

Although this workbook has been designed primarily for use by a class that is slightly beyond the midpoint in an introductory grammar, some instructors may prefer to schedule the course to finish the introductory grammar in time to allow the final six weeks or so of class to be devoted solely to translating 1 John and working through this study guide.

This guide to the study of 1 John can also be used by individuals who are studying Greek on their own and have access to a theological library. Individuals are encouraged before beginning one of the twenty-five assignments to make note of and collect the volumes cited in the particular assignment being studied. Having a copy of the Greek New Testament and these reference works close at hand, they can proceed to research the questions.

Although this workbook was produced primarily to benefit students of elementary Greek grammar, it can also serve to enlighten and sharpen the skills of students of intermediate Greek grammar. The authors hope that this present edition will be of value to all students of New Testament Greek who wish to study 1 John in the original language.

Publications are possible only with the help of many along the way. Over the years our students at Gordon-Conwell Theological Seminary (1957–1960), Barrington College (1963–1971), Gordon College (1971–present), and the Utah Institute for Biblical Studies (1984–present; recently renamed Salt Lake Seminary) have earned much appreciation on our part. They have provided us with helpful criticism and suggestions as together we have worked through most of these materials in the classroom setting. Many ideas shared by these students have been incorporated in the present edition.

A Workbook for New Testament Greek: Grammar and Exegesis in First John represents a thorough revision, updating, and expansion of Marvin R. Wilson's earlier (1979) publication. As for this present jointly authored volume, Chris Alex Vlachos did the major work of drafting the revision (including a thorough updating of the manuscript) and Marvin R. Wilson served as main editor and project overseer. In addition, several students have made valuable contributions. The authors wish to thank Pat Pitcher of Salt Lake City, Utah, for the tedious task she performed in proofreading the draft of this work. The authors also express their appreciation to Andrew Ziegler of Campbell, California, for preparing the ANALYTICAL LEXICON found in the back of this book. Finally, the authors acknowledge with considerable gratitude the skillful work of graduate student Rebecca Gates, who as research assistant helped expedite the preparation of the manuscript for publication.

ABBREVIATIONS

1. General Abbreviations

acc.	accusative	masc.	masculine
act.	active	mg	margin
adj.	adjective	mid.	middle
adv.	adverb	ms(s).	manuscript(s)
aor.	aorist	n.	note
ca.	about, approximately	neut.	neuter
cent.	century	nom.	nominative
cf.	compare	NIV	New International Version
comp.	comparative		
cond.	conditional	NKJV	New King James Version
conj.	conjunction		
dat.	dative	NT	New Testament
decl.	declension	pass.	passive
ed.	edition	perf.	perfect
ed(s).	editor(s)	periphr.	periphrastic (tense)
e.g.	for example	pl.	plural
fem.	feminine	pluperf.	pluperfect
fut.	future	prep.	preposition
gen.	genitive	pres.	present
i.e.	in other words	pron.	pronoun
impf.	imperfect	ptcp.	participle
impv.	imperative	rel.	relative
indef.	indefinite	sg.	singular
indic.	indicative	subj.	subjunctive
indecl.	indeclinable	s.v.	under the word
infin.	infinitive	vb.	verb
instr.	instrumental	v(v).	verse(s)
interrog.	interrogative	voc.	vocative
KJV	King James Version	vol(s).	volume(s)
LXX	Septuagint		

2. Abbreviations for Works Frequently Cited

ABD   David Noel Freedman, ed. *The Anchor Bible Dictionary.* 6 vols. New York: Doubleday, 1992.

BAGD   W. Bauer. *A Greek-English Lexicon of the New Testament and Other Early Christian Literature.* 2d ed. Translated by W. F. Arndt and F. W. Gingrich. Revised and edited by F. W. Danker. Chicago: University of Chicago Press, 1979.

BDF   F. Blass and A. Debrunner. *A Greek Grammar of the New Testament.* Translated and edited by R. W. Funk. Chicago: University of Chicago Press, 1961.

EDNT   Horst Balz and Gerhard Schneider, eds. *Exegetical Dictionary of the New Testament.* 3 vols. Grand Rapids: Eerdmans, 1993.

GNT   Barbara Aland, Kurt Aland, Johannes Karavidopoulos, Carlo M. Martini, and Bruce Metzger, eds. *The Greek New Testament.* 4th rev. ed. Stuttgart: Deutsche Bibelgesellschaft and United Bible Societies, 1993.

ISBE   Geoffrey W. Bromiley, ed. *The International Standard Bible Encyclopedia.* 4 vols. Grand Rapids: Eerdmans, 1988.

NA^{27} Barbara Aland, Kurt Aland, Johannes Karavidopoulos, Carlo M. Martini, and Bruce Metzger, eds. *Novum Testamentum Graece.* 27th ed. Stuttgart: Deutsche Bibelgesellschaft, 1993.

NIDNTT   Colin Brown, ed. *The New International Dictionary of New Testament Theology.* 4 vols. Grand Rapids: Zondervan, 1975–1986.

TDNT   Gerhard Kittel and Gerhard Friedrich, eds. *Theological Dictionary of the New Testament.* 10 vols. Translated by G. W. Bromiley. Grand Rapids: Eerdmans, 1964–1976.

INTRODUCTION TO FIRST JOHN

The First Letter of John is anonymous but has traditionally been attributed to John the apostle, author of the Fourth Gospel. This was the identification made by Irenaeus (ca. A.D. 140–203), Clement of Alexandria (ca. A.D. 155–215), Tertullian (ca. A.D. 150–222), and Origen (ca. A.D. 185–253).

When the evidence is weighed, this early tradition seems to be a reasonable hypothesis. The writer presents himself as an eyewitness of Jesus (1:1–4; 4:14). In addition, he addresses his readers in such warm and loving tones as "little children" (2:1, 18; 3:7). These tender, fatherly expressions may well have come from an old man. Tradition informs us John's later years were spent in Ephesus from where he penned the letter near, or in, the last decade of the first century.

That the author of the letter is in all probability John the apostle is also borne out by its close similarity in style and vocabulary to the Fourth Gospel, which, in light of John 21:20–24 and the earlier tradition of the church, was likely written by this apostle. (For a discussion of Johannine authorship of the Fourth Gospel, see D. A. Carson, *The Gospel According to John* [Grand Rapids: Eerdmans, 1991], 68–81.) The sentence structure in both is simple and the style repetitive. Both employ contrasting figures, such as light and darkness, life and death, truth and lies, love and hate. Expressions in 1 John similar to those of the Fourth Gospel include "abide," "do the truth," "Spirit of truth," "overcome the world," "begotten of God," "eternal life," "lay down one's life," "light," "love," "new commandment," "Paraclete," etc. Note the following parallels:

1 John	Gospel of John
1:1	1:1, 14
1:4	16:24
1:6–7	3:19–21
2:1	14:16
2:7	13:34–35
2:24	15:5
3:8	8:44
3:14	5:24
4:6	8:47
4:6	16:13
4:9	1:14, 18; 3:16
5:5	16:33
5:9	5:32, 37
5:12–13	3:36
5:18	3:3, 16

Moreover, the Gospel and the Epistle share certain grammatical features. Among these are the relative scarcity of particles, the common use of πᾶς ὁ with the participle (John 3:8, 15, 16; etc. and 1 John 3:4; 5:1; etc.) and πᾶν ὅ with a finite verb or πᾶν τό with the participle (John 6:37, 39; 15:2; 1 John 2:16; 5:4), the use of the demonstrative pronoun (οὗτος) to introduce a subordinate clause (John 3:19; 5:16; 9:30; 13:35; 1 John 2:3; 3:1; 4:9; 5:9; etc.), and the occurrences of καθὼς . . . καί (John 13:15; 1 John 2:18), οὐ καθώς (John 6:58; 1 John 3:12), ἀλλ' ἵνα (John 1:8; 9:3; 1 John 2:19) and καὶ . . . δέ (John 6:51; 8:16; 15:27; 1 John 1:3). This workbook will therefore assume Johannine authorship of 1 John. Readers who prefer other conclusions are asked to accept the use of "John" for "the author" for the sake of convenience and consistency.

John's First Epistle appears to be more in the form of a sermon than a letter. It may be observed that the usual introductory address and farewell greetings are not found. In addition, there is no historical or geographical information, and apart from mention of the Lord, this writing lacks any contemporary personal names. Although such verses as 1 John 2:12–14, 19; 3:1; 5:13 make it clear that the letter was addressed to Christians, the omission of any personal references probably indicates that the document was intended to circulate as a general letter among believers at large. Clement of Alexandria indicates that John served the various churches scattered throughout the province of Asia (in modern Turkey). It may be assumed, therefore, that 1 John was sent to the churches of that province.

The immediate historical occasion of this letter of John was apparently the spread of an early form of what later became known as Gnosticism. The Gnostics held to a dualism that viewed matter as evil and spirit as good. A good God would be totally separate from the evil world of flesh and matter. Thus God, the Gnostics taught, could not have taken upon himself human flesh. Some forms of Gnosticism taught that Jesus only *seemed* to have taken on a body, a view called Docetism, from the Greek word δοκέω ("seem"). Others maintained that the divine Christ joined the human Jesus at his baptism and left him before his death. This later view was held by Cerinthus. Perhaps one or both of these views provided the backdrop to 1:1, 3; 2:22; 4:2–3 where John stresses that Jesus Christ was God's Son come in the flesh. For John, there was no cosmic dualism. In Jesus Christ, the divine and the human were one person. He was fully God and fully man.

Gnostics also taught that salvation, which for them meant escape from the body, was achieved not through faith in Christ but through a special knowledge (the Greek word for "knowledge" is γνῶσις, hence *Gnosticism*). John's repeated references to "knowledge" (forty occurrences of γινώσκω and οἶδα in the epistle) and his desire that believers in Christ would "know" that their salvation was certain (5:13) may have been aimed at this viewpoint. Some Gnostics also believed that immorality was inconsequential since matter, not the breaking of God's law, was considered to be evil. John's strong emphasis in 3:8–10 and elsewhere against sin may have been aimed at this philosophically based licentiousness.

It appears probable, therefore, that the false teachers whom John sought to expose (2:26) were early or proto-Gnostics. Although the general characteristics of their teaching can be fairly well reconstructed from John's response, it is impossible to identify the opponents precisely.

John's letter is difficult to outline. He works with a number of different themes such as love (ἀγάπη), sin (ἁμαρτία), the world (κόσμος), knowledge (γνῶσις), and truth (ἀλήθεια). These themes are repeated throughout the book rather than treated in logical sequence. As mentioned, John displays contrast by using antithetical concepts. In other places (e.g., 1:6–10), John's style is highly Semitic as seen in his use of parallelism and restatement of key ideas.

The theology of John is far from theoretical. He seeks to bring his readers into the reality of a close personal experience with the living God. His concern is emphatic: "that you may know him who is true" (5:20). The Word of Life has become incarnate in the Son of God. It is John's desire that the Word of Life now be fleshed out in each believer.

For further information on the background of the First Letter of John see the commentaries listed in the bibliography. Especially helpful are Stott and Johnson for the beginning student of John's epistle, and Marshall and Smalley for those on an intermediate level. Brown and Schnackenburg are for the advanced student.

The Fleshed-Out Life
1 John 1:1–4

VOCABULARY

ὅ, neut. nom. sg. of ὅς, ἥ, ὅ, *that which, what.* Cf. John 4:22. For declension see Mounce, *Basics*, §14.7.

ἀπ᾽ ἀρχῆς, *from the very beginning.* See BAGD, s.v. ἀρχή 1.c.

ἀκηκόαμεν, 2d perf. indic. act. 1st pl. of ἀκούω, *we have heard*

ἑωράκαμεν, perf. indic. act. 1st pl. of ὁράω, *we have seen*

ὀφθαλμοῖς, instr. dat., *with our eyes*

ἐθεασάμεθα, aor. indic. mid. 1st pl. of θεάομαι, *we beheld, saw, looked at, viewed,* the word from which the English word "theater" comes. It may connote seeing with physical eyes in such a way that supernatural insight is gained. See BAGD, s.v. θεάομαι 2. For the possible distinction between ὁράω and θεάομαι, see Vincent, *Writings of John,* 59.

χεῖρες, 3d decl. fem. nom. pl. of χείρ, χειρός, *hands*

ἐψηλάφησαν, aor. indic. act. 3d pl. of ψηλαφάω, *they felt, touched, handled,* establishing the corporeality and historicity of the life-giving Word. See *EDNT* 3:499–500.

ἐφανερώθη, aor. indic. pass. 3d sg. of φανερόω, *it became visible, was revealed, was made known*

μαρτυρέω, *witness, bear witness, testify, be a witness*

ἀπαγγέλλω, *announce, declare, report, proclaim.* With the possible focus on the source from which (ἀπό) the information comes.

αἰώνιον, fem. acc. sg. of αἰώνιος, -ον, *eternal, everlasting*

ἥτις, qualitative rel. pron. fem. nom. sg., *which.* Found in lexicons under ὅστις (masc. nom. sg.).

πρός, prep. with acc., *with, in company with.* See BAGD, s.v. πρός 7; *NIDNTT* 3:1204–5.

πατέρα, 3d decl. masc. acc. sg. of πατήρ, πατρός, *father*

κοινωνία, -ας, ἡ, *fellowship, participation, communion, sharing.* See Marshall, *Epistles,* 104.

ἔχητε, pres. subj. act. 2d pl. of ἔχω, *[that] you may have* ἡμέτερος, -α, -ον, possessive adj. used for emphasis, *belonging to us, our.* See Greenlee, *Exegetical Grammar,* 69.

ᾖ πεπληρωμένη, perf. periphr. subj. pass. 3d sg. from πληρόω, *may be made full, complete.* For the basic meaning of a periphrastic participial construction, see Mounce, *Basics,* §30.10.

QUESTIONS

1. How many times does ψηλαφάω occur in the Greek New Testament? (See Kohlenberger, Goodrick, and Swanson, *Exhaustive Concordance.*) Which one of these passages sheds direct light on John's use in v. 1? Why?

   4x   Luke 24:39

2. Why does John emphasize that Christ was tangible and visible? What rival teaching was he possibly combating? (See Marshall, *Epistles,* 101 n. 9.)

   Docetism

3. What verbal and thematic parallels exist between τὴν ζωὴν τὴν αἰώνιον ἥτις ἦν πρὸς τὸν πατέρα (v. 2) and John 1:1b (καὶ ὁ λόγος ἦν πρὸς τὸν θεόν)? What do these parallels imply about the personal nature of the ζωὴ αἰώνιος of v. 2? (Cf. John 1:4, 11:25; 14:6.) What do they imply about its divine nature? (See Smalley, *1, 2, 3 John,* 10–11.)

4. What is the significance of the tense of ἀκηκόαμεν and ἐωράκαμεν in vv. 1–3? (See Wuest, *Expanded Translation*, 565.) What is the significance of the tense of μαρτυροῦμεν and ἀπαγγέλλομεν (vv. 2, 3)?

5. Is the adjective αἰώνιον in v. 2 in the attributive or the predicative position? What is the significance of the repetition of article? What is the significance of the position of the adjective? (See Young, *Intermediate NT Greek*, 81; Robertson, *Grammar*, 776; Wallace, *Grammar*, 306.)

6. In v. 3 why does John use the phrase κοινωνίαν ἔχητε instead of κοινωνεῖτε? (See Westcott, *Epistles*, 12.)

7. To what does ταῦτα (v. 4) refer?

8. What meaning does ἡμεῖς add to v. 4? (See BDF §280.)

FOR FURTHER STUDY

1. What phases in the existence of the Son does John dramatically unfold in vv. 1–3 as he moves from impersonal neuter pronouns describing Christ ("that which") to verbs of personal encounter (hearing, seeing, feeling) and finally identifies and proclaims him? How does this movement of thought highlight the transcendence and immanence of Christ?

2. According to Greenlee, anything that precedes the verb (except for words that grammatically *must* stand first) should usually be considered emphatic (*Exegetical Grammar*, 68; for a more detailed discussion of word order, see Young, *Intermediate NT Greek*, 214–18). What words do you find being emphasized by John in vv. 1–4?

3. Find the Greek words in this assignment from which the following English words derive: aeon, architect, zodiac, logic, martyr, ophthalmology, chiropractic, paternal, phantom.

Walking in the Light
1 John 1:5–7

VOCABULARY

ἀγγελία, -ας, ἡ, *message, news*

ἀναγγέλλω, *announce, declare, report, proclaim,* with the possible emphasis on the bringing of the message *up* or *back* (ἀνά) to the one who receives it. A directional connotation in ἀναγγέλλω (and ἀπαγγέλλω), however, may not be intended. (See Brown, *Epistles*, 194.)

ὅτι, conj., *that, because.* May mark the beginning of direct discourse.

φῶς, 3d decl. neut. nom. sg. of φῶς, φωτός, *light, that which illuminates*

σκοτία, -ας, ἡ, *darkness.* May be used figuratively "of the darkening of the mind or spirit, of ignorance in moral and religious matters. . . . Especially in Johannine usage as a category including everything that is at enmity with God, earthly and demonic" (BAGD, s.v. σκοτία 2).

οὐδεμία, fem. nom. sg. of the 1st and 3d decl. adj. οὐδείς, οὐδεμία, οὐδέν, *not one (bit)*

ἐάν, combination of εἰ plus ἄν, *if.* Used with the subjunctive to express a hypothetical condition. (See Dana and Mantey, *Manual Grammar*, §216.)

εἴπωμεν, 2d aor. subj. act. 1st pl. of λέγω, *[if] we say.* Note how vv. 6, 8, and 10 begin with ἐὰν εἴπωμεν, an example of a rhetorical device utilizing repetition known as *anaphora* (Gk. ἀναφορά, "a carrying back").

σκότει, 3d decl. neut. dat. sg. of σκότος, σκότους, *darkness.* (It is the opposite of φῶς.) There is no difference in meaning between σκοτία and σκότος.

περιπατῶμεν, pres. subj. act. 1st pl. of περιπατέω, *[if] we walk*

ψεύδομαι, *lie, deceive by telling lies*

ὡς, adv., *as*

αἷμα, 3d decl. neut. nom. sg. of αἷμα, αἵματος, *blood.* For the declension of third declension neuter nouns in -μα, see Wenham, *Elements*, 118.

καθαρίζω, *cleanse, make clean*

πάσης, fem. gen. sg. of the 1st and 3d decl. adj. πᾶς, πᾶσα, πᾶν, *all, every.* For complete declension see Moulton and Howard, *Accidence*, 158.

QUESTIONS

1. There are two negatives in v. 5, οὐκ and οὐδεμία. In NT Greek do two negatives cancel each other out? (See Wenham, *Elements*, 128; Young, *Intermediate NT Greek*, 203.)

2. Occasionally, a word placed last in a sentence or clause is being stressed. (See Greenlee, *Exegetical Grammar*, 68.) Does this appear to be the case with οὐδεμία in its clause (v. 5)?

3. How is ὅτι used in v. 5? (See BAGD, s.v. ὅτι 1.a.) How is ὅτι used in v. 6? (Ibid., 1.b.α; BDF §397.3.)

4. According to Kohlenberger, Goodrick, and Swanson, *Exhaustive Concordance*, how many times does φῶς (v. 5) occur in 1 John? In how many of these occurrences is φῶς anarthrous (without the article)? What is often being emphasized when a noun is anarthrous? (See Dana and Mantey, *Manual Grammar*, §149.) According to Wallace (*Grammar*, 262), what idea is normally conveyed by an anarthrous pre-verbal predicate nominative? How would this observation affect your understanding of φῶς in v. 5? Would it be best translated as "a light," "the light," or "light"? (See also 1 John 4:8; John 1:1, 14.)

5. Again utilizing Kohlenberger, Goodrick, and Swanson, *Exhaustive Concordance*, examine the New Testament contexts in which κοινωνία (v. 5) occurs. In the New Testament is the term ever used to characterize those who walk in darkness and who do not practice the truth? (See Barclay, *NT Words*, 173–76.)

6. What does the tense of καθαρίζει (v. 7) imply about the sanctification of the believer?

FOR FURTHER STUDY

1. Note carefully the verbal and thematic parallels and contrasts in 1 John 1:6–10 below (see ASSIGNMENT 3 for vocabulary helps for vv. 8–10). On the basis of these parallels and contrasts, what do "walking in the darkness" and "walking in the light" primarily entail?

⁶ Ἐὰν εἴπωμεν ὅτι κοινωνίαν ἔχομεν μετ' αὐτοῦ καὶ ἐν τῷ σκότει
  περιπατῶμεν,
   ψευδόμεθα καὶ οὐ ποιοῦμεν τὴν ἀλήθειαν·

⁷ ἐὰν δὲ ἐν τῷ φωτὶ περιπατῶμεν ὡς αὐτός ἐστιν ἐν τῷ φωτί,
   κοινωνίαν ἔχομεν μετ' ἀλλήλων καὶ τὸ αἷμα Ἰησοῦ τοῦ υἱοῦ αὐτοῦ
   καθαρίζει ἡμᾶς ἀπὸ πάσης ἁμαρτίας.

⁸ ἐὰν εἴπωμεν ὅτι ἁμαρτίαν οὐκ ἔχομεν,
   ἑαυτοὺς πλανῶμεν καὶ ἡ ἀλήθεια οὐκ ἔστιν ἐν ἡμῖν.

⁹ ἐὰν ὁμολογῶμεν τὰς ἁμαρτίας ἡμῶν,
   πιστός ἐστιν καὶ δίκαιος, ἵνα ἀφῇ ἡμῖν τὰς ἁμαρτίας καὶ καθαρίσῃ
   ἡμᾶς ἀπὸ πάσης ἀδικίας.

¹⁰ ἐὰν εἴπωμεν ὅτι οὐχ ἡμαρτήκαμεν,
   ψεύστην ποιοῦμεν αὐτὸν καὶ ὁ λόγος αὐτοῦ οὐκ ἔστιν ἐν ἡμῖν.

2. What kind of predicate nominative is φῶς in v. 5 (cf. 1 John 4:8; John 4:24)? (See Wallace, *Grammar*, 264–65.) What, according to Wallace (*Grammar*, 264 n. 24), is a good way to determine whether a predicate nominative is definite (i.e., stressing the noun's identity) rather than qualitative (i.e., stressing the noun's nature or essence)? Translate the verse in a way that stresses the idea conveyed by the predicate noun in this particular sentence structure.

----

3. The Bible depicts one's daily life of faith in terms of a journey or pilgrimage. Religion was the way one chose to "walk." Who were the first two persons who walked with God? (See Gen 5:2; 6:9.) Read Ps 1:6; 119:105; Prov 3:6; and Mic 6:8. Compare these Old Testament texts to Matt 7:13–14; John 14:6; Acts 9:2; 19:9, 23; Gal 5:16; and 1 John 1:6–7. Now discuss whether or not you agree with the following: Some would define religion as a system of ethics, a code of conduct, an ideology, or a creed. The Bible, however, defines religion primarily as a faith-love relationship with the living God, with whom one "walks" in fellowship on the path of light (vv. 5–7).

4. Find the Greek words in this assignment from which the following English words derive: angel, pseudo, photography, hematology, catharsis.

VOCABULARY

πλανῶμεν, pres. indic. act. 1st pl. of πλανάω, *we mislead, lead astray, deceive.* From the root of this word comes the English word, "planet," i.e., "a wandering star."

ὁμολογῶμεν, pres. subj. act. 1st pl. of ὁμολογέω, *[if] we confess, acknowledge, admit, declare publicly.* From ὁμός, "the same" and λέγω, "to say," i.e., "to say the same thing as another," and therefore, "to admit the truth of an accusation." See *NIDNTT* 1:344.

ἵνα, *to.* Occurring (with few exceptions) with the subjunctive mood primarily to express purpose, but can also be used to introduce a noun clause, to modify certain nouns and adjectives, or, as here, to express result. (See BDF, §391.5; BAGD, s.v. ἵνα II.2.)

ἀφῇ, 2d aor. subj. act. 3d sg. of ἀφίημι, *[to] forgive, send away, let go.* For a brief study of this term, see Barclay, *NT Words,* 125.

καθαρίσῃ, aor. subj. act. 3d sing. of καθαρίζω, *[to] cleanse*

ἀδικία, -ας, ἡ, *unrighteousness, injustice, wrong*

ἡμαρτήκαμεν, perf. indic. act. 1st pl. of ἁμαρτάνω, *we have [not] sinned*

ψεύστης, -ου, ὁ, *liar*

QUESTIONS

1. According to Smalley (*1, 2, 3 John*, 29), does the phrase ἁμαρτία ἔχειν refer primarily to individual acts of sin or to a sinful condition? (See also BAGD, s.v. ἁμαρτία 2; Westcott, *Epistles*, 22.) Based on your answer how would you translate v. 8?

2. What part of speech is ἑαυτούς (v. 8)? (See Machen, *NT Greek for Beginners*, §339–42; Wenham, *Elements*, 61.) What is its antecedent in this verse? (See Zerwick, *Biblical Greek*, §209.)

3. How does the use of ὁμολογέω in v. 9 contrast with λέγω in vv. 6, 8, 10? What is the difference between confessing something and merely saying something?

4. What kind of action expressed is by the perfect tense? (See Wallace, *Greek Grammar*, 573–74.) What, if anything, does the tense of ἡμαρτήκαμεν (v. 10) suggest regarding the possibility of achieving sinless perfection in this life?

5. How do the accusatives ψεύστην and αὐτόν function in v. 10? (See Brooks and Winbery, *Syntax*, 51–52.) Which noun is in the emphatic position in relation to the verb?

6. How does the use of the term λόγος in v. 10 differ from its use in v. 1? (See BAGD, s.v. λόγος, if you need help; for a variety of meanings that λόγος carries in ancient Greek literature, see *ABD* 4:348–56.)

7. According to Porter (*Idioms*, 263), what might be the significance of the contrasting present and aorist subjunctives in vv. 6–10?

FOR FURTHER STUDY

1. Many theologians would agree that the capacity of every human to sin is one of the most empirically verifiable doctrines of the Christian faith. In regard to sin John warns believers about the problem of self-deception and the need to admit the truth about themselves (v. 8). In this vein, T. S. Eliot has observed that telling the truth is extraordinarily difficult at times because we are creatures who cannot bear too much reality. Discuss self-deception in the context of vv. 8–10 and also in light of Eliot's insight.

2. Is John referring in v. 9 to the initial act of repentance and confession that occurs at conversion or to the ongoing practice of confession of sins throughout the Christian's life? Does the tense of ὁμολογῶμεν help answer the question?

3. How would the fact that God is πιστός and δίκαιος (v. 9) bring assurance to the conscience of the penitent Christian? (See Stott, *Letters of John*, 82–83.)

God's Provision for Sin
1 John 2:1–6

VOCABULARY

τεκνίον, -ου, τό, *little child.* The diminutive of τέκνον as a term of affection; used by Jesus in John 13:33.

ἁμάρτητε, 2d aor. subj. act. 2d pl. of ἁμαρτάνω, *[that] you [might not] sin*

τις, indef. pron. masc. nom. sg. of τις, τι, *someone, a certain one, anyone.* For declension see Mounce, *Basics,* 342.

παράκλητος, -ου, ὁ, *advocate, intercessor, helper.* Cf. John 14:16, 26; 15:26; 16:7. See Louw and Nida, *Lexicon,* §35.16.

ἱλασμός, -οῦ, ὁ, *propitiation, expiation; sin-offering.* See BAGD, s.v., and *ISBE* 3:1004–5.

μόνον, adv., *only*

ὅλος, -η, -ον, *whole, all.* The English word "holocaust" is derived from ὅλος (ὅλος, "whole," and καυστός, "burnt," i.e., "a whole burnt offering").

ἐγνώκαμεν, perf. indic. act. 1st pl. of γινώσκω, *we have come to know*

τηρῶμεν, pres. subj. act. 1st pl. of τηρέω, *[if] we keep*

λέγων, pres. ptcp. act. masc. nom. sg. of λέγω, *[the one who] says, claims*

τηρῶν, pres. ptcp. act. masc. nom. sg. of τηρέω, *[the one who does not] keep*

ὅς . . . ἄν, cond./indef. rel. clause, *whoever [keeps].* See Machen, *NT Greek for Beginners,* §400; Wenham, *Elements,* 160.

ἀληθῶς, adv., *truly, surely*

τετελείωται, perf. indic. pass. 3d sg. of τελειόω, *it is completed, finished*

μένειν, pres. infin. act. of μένω, *to remain, abide*

ὀφείλω, *owe, be indebted, be obligated.* With the infinitive, as in 1 John 2:6: "I ought, must."

καθώς, adv., *just as*

[οὕτως], adv., *thus, so, in this way.* The brackets in our critical editions indicate uncertainty as to whether or not the enclosed word is part of the original text.

περιπατεῖν, pres. infin. act. of περιπατέω, *to walk*

QUESTIONS

1. Who is the παράκλητος of v. 1? What special meaning does this term have in this context? (See Barclay, *NT Words*, 215–22; for a discussion of this word and further reading on this topic, see *ABD* 5:152–54.)

2. What special nuance does περί (v. 2) convey when used along with ἁμαρτία? (See BAGD, s.v. περί 1.g; see also Porter, *Idioms*, 170.)

3. What difference in meaning is conveyed by the change of tense in John's statement, γινώσκομεν ὅτι ἐγνώκαμεν αὐτόν (v. 3)?

4. How does the participle λέγων function syntactically in vv. 4 and 6? (See Mounce, *Basics*, §29.7–8; Wallace, *Grammar*, 619–21.)

5. How does Granville Sharp's rule apply to v. 4? (See Brooks and Winbery, *Syntax*, 76; for a more thorough discussion of this rule, see Wallace, *Grammar*, 270–90.)

6. What words at the beginning of v. 3 and the end of v. 5 form an *inclusio* or bracket to the argument of vv. 3–5? What other verbal or thematic parallels are found between vv. 3 and 5?

7. Verse 6 may initially be baffling to students of New Testament Greek. One of the difficulties is that the verb ὀφείλει is separated from its complementary infinitive (περιπατεῖν) by the words καθὼς ἐκεῖνος περιεπάτησεν καὶ αὐτὸς [οὕτως]. The placement of this cluster of words before the infinitive gives it an emphatic position in the sentence. Translate the verse out loud placing emphasis on these intervening words. Make special note of the emphatic use of the terms ἐκεῖνος and αὐτός. (See Greenlee, *Exegetical Grammar*, 69.)

8. Zerwick and Grosvenor identify περιεπάτησεν (v. 6) as a constative (global) aorist (*Grammatical Analysis*, 727). How does a constative or global aorist present the action of the verb? (See Zerwick, *Biblical Greek*, §253; Brooks and Winbery, *Syntax*, 99.)

FOR FURTHER STUDY

1. The word "exegesis" is an important term for any student of biblical Greek. It involves a detailed inductive analysis of the passage being studied. The goal of exegesis is to arrive at the proper meaning or interpretation of the passage so that useful application may be made of its teaching. A thorough exegesis entails (1) a determination of the correct text and translation, (2) a careful study of the historical background and cultural context, (3) an outline of the structure or flow of the passage, breaking it down into its various units of thought, (4) a grammatical, syntactical study of the passage with an analysis of any key words, (5) a study of the passage in its context in relation to the chapter, book, group of writings, and Testament where it is found, and (6) an existential application of the passage to contemporary faith and life. (See Fee, *Exegesis*, 32–61, for a more thorough process.)

   Though this exegetical process is necessary for any comprehensive study of a passage, an abbreviated procedure that entails examining the (1) roots, (2) forms, (3) syntax, and (4) context can be a useful exercise for students. Using this simpler procedure, decide whether or not John is teaching the possibility of sinless perfection in 1 John 2:1. Note the root meaning of ἁμαρτάνω and its tense form, then examine the syntax and the immediate context for limitations on John's meaning.

2. Locate the use of ἱλασμός in the LXX (the Greek Old Testament) utilizing Hatch and Redpath's *Concordance to the Septuagint*. Read a few of the passages. How does the Old Testament context of this word add to your own understanding of its use in v. 2?

3. How many times does the term γινώσκω (v. 3) occur in 1 John? (See Kohlenberger, Goodrick, and Swanson, *Exhaustive Concordance.*) On the basis of this emphasis on "knowledge," to what religious viewpoint was John perhaps responding? (See Smalley, *1, 2, 3 John,* 44–45.) According to Smalley, how does John counter this way of thinking?

_____

_____

_____

_____

_____

A Commandment Both Old and New
1 John 2:7–11

VOCABULARY

ἀγαπητός, -ή, -όν, *beloved*

καινός, -ή, -όν, *new, fresh, unused* (with reference to quality, not chronology). See Trench, *Synonyms*, 219–25.

παλαιός, -ά, -όν, *old, ancient*

πάλιν, adv., *again, once more*

ἀληθές, neut. nom. sg. of the 3d decl. adj. ἀληθής, ἀληθές, *true*. For declension see Wenham, *Elements*, 123.

παράγεται, pres. indic. pass. 3d sg. of παράγω, *it is passing away, disappearing, caused to pass away*

ἀληθινός, -ή, -όν, *real, true, genuine, dependable*. See Trench, *Synonyms*, 26–30, for a discussion of the distinctions between ἀληθινός and ἀληθής.

ἤδη, adv., *now, already, by this time*

φαίνω, *give light, shine*

εἶναι, pres. infin. act. of εἰμί, *to be*

μισῶν, pres. ptcp. act. masc. nom. sg. of μισέω, *[the one who] hates*

ἕως, conj., *until*

ἄρτι, adv., *now, just now, just at this moment, at the present time*

ἀγαπῶν, pres. ptcp. act. masc. nom. sg. of ἀγαπάω, *[the one who] loves*. See *NIDNTT* 2:538–51 for a study of the Greek terms for "love."

σκάνδαλον, -ου, τό, *a stumbling block, cause of sin, something that gives offense*

οἶδεν, 2d perf. indic. act. 3d sg. of οἶδα, *he [does not] know*. It is used as a present. Forms of οἶδα account for over one-fourth of all perfects in the New Testament.

ποῦ, interrog. adv., *where?* It is used in 1 John 2:11 in an indirect question.

ὑπάγω, *go away, depart, leave*

ἐτύφλωσεν, aor. indic. act. 3d sg. of τυφλόω, *it blinded, made blind, deprived of sight*

QUESTIONS

1. What does the tense of εἴχετε (v. 7) emphasize about the existence of the old commandment? (For the identification of this use of the imperfect see Young, *Intermediate NT Greek*, 115.)

_____

_____

_____

2. A relative pronoun agrees with its antecedent in gender and number. Is ἐντολή the antecedent of ὅ in v. 8? If not, to what does ὅ refer? (See Vincent, *Writings of John*, 331; Smalley, *1, 2, 3 John*, 56–57; Moule, *Idiom Book*, 130–31.)

_____

_____

_____

3. How is ὅτι used in v. 8?

_____

_____

4. What does the tense of παράγεται connote in v. 8? (See Rogers and Rogers, *New Linguistic and Exegetical Key*, 593.)

_____

_____

5. How should καί be translated in v. 9? (See Chamberlain, *Exegetical Grammar*, 149.)

_____

_____

_____

6. Does the phrase ἐν αὐτῷ in v. 10 refer to the believer ("in *him*") or to the light in which the believer remains ("in *it*")? (See v. 11 and John 11:9.)

_____

_____

7. What idea is brought out more forcefully by the use of the verb ὑπάγω in v. 11 than would be conveyed by ἔρχομαι or πορεύομαι? (See Rogers and Rogers, *New Linguistic and Exegetical Key*, 593.)

_____

_____

8. What three types of contract verb are found in vv. 10–11? Review the rules of contraction for vowels. (See Machen, *NT Greek for Beginners*, §314–16; Wenham, *Elements*, 236, 238, 240; Mounce, *Basics*, 329.)

_____

_____

_____

For Further Study

1. In an unabridged dictionary of the English language, look up the etymology and meanings of the following words: misanthrope, palimpsest, scandal, typhlosis. Identify the Greek word in 1 John 2:7–11 from which each term is derived.

_____

_____

2. What is the "old commandment" (v. 7) and why is it also a "new commandment" (v. 8)? How can something be both old and new?

_____

_____

3. An effective aspect of John's literary style is his use of opposite terms or antonyms. Point out at least three pairs of antonyms in vv. 7–11.

_____

_____

_____

4. Words, whether in English or Greek, have meaning only in context. What is the probable meaning of ἀδελφός in the context of vv. 9–11 and of the epistle as a whole? What other meanings could this term convey? (See the five meanings listed in BAGD, s.v. ἀδελφός.)

_____

_____

_____

5. In Hatch and Redpath's *Concordance to the Septuagint,* locate and read several passages where σκάνδαλον (v. 10) occurs. What two shades of meaning can you discern? Can both be applicable in the context of 1 John 2:10? (See Barclay, *NT Words,* 255–58; Smalley, *1, 2, 3 John,* 62.)

_____

_____

_____

A Word for the Whole Family
1 John 2:12–14

VOCABULARY

ἀφέωνται, perf. indic. pass. 3d pl. of ἀφίημι, *they have been forgiven*

ὄνομα, ὀνόματος, τό, *name*

νεανίσκος, -ου, ὁ, *young man, youth*

νενικήκατε, perf. indic. act. 2d pl. of νικάω, *you have conquered, over-*
come, won the victory

παιδίον, -ου, τό, *child, little child.* The root of this noun is related to
the English word "pedagogy"; cf. παῖς, *boy, youth.*

ἰσχυρός, -ά, -όν, *powerful, mighty, strong*

QUESTIONS

1. Discuss the case and use of τεκνία (v. 12).

2. How is the conjunction ὅτι used in vv. 12–14? (See Wenham,
   Elements, 106 [1].)

3. Are the forgiveness spoken of in v. 12 and the victory viewed in v. 13 permanent realities? Why? (See Haas, DeJonge, and Swellengrebel, *Translator's Handbook*, 55.)

4. As what part of speech is πονηρόν being used in vv. 13–14? (See Young, *Intermediate NT Greek*, 82.)

5. How does the phrase τὸν ἀπ' ἀρχῆς function in vv. 13 and 14? (See Hewett, *Grammar*, 51; Wallace, *Grammar*, 236.) To whom does the phrase refer? (Cf. 1:1.)

6. Verse 14 contains three instances of the "epistolary aorist" (ἔγραψα). From what viewpoint does an epistolary aorist view the action conveyed in the verb? (See Burton, *Syntax*, §44; Moule, *Idiom Book*, 12.)

FOR FURTHER STUDY

1. The root of νικάω (νίκη) has given rise to such words as the Greek deity of victory, Nike (cf. the name of a well-known company that manufactures sneakers!) and the city of Nicea (Nicene Creed). What words found in the New Testament are also related to this root? (See Greenlee, *Morpheme Lexicon*, 89.)

2. In v. 12 John refers to forgiveness διὰ τὸ ὄνομα αὐτοῦ. (Cf. 3:23; 5:13.) Where else do references to Christ's name occur in Johannine literature, and what do these references to his name signify? (See Brown, *Epistles*, 302–303.)

3. John addresses his adult readers as τεκνία (v. 12) and παιδία (v. 14), "little children." Is the term one of insult or affection? Why?

4. In vv. 13–14 John uses the word πατέρες, "fathers," but there is a certain ambiguity as to how this word is to be understood. In the context of this epistle, what are some of the possible ways of interpreting the term and which interpretation do you favor? Why? (For a discussion of this passage, see Marshall, *Epistles*, 134–41.)

5. What is the "word of God" (ὁ λόγος τοῦ θεοῦ) that lives in these early believers (v. 14)? Why is this abiding presence of the word also important for today's church as a vital resource for overcoming sin? What can one learn in this regard from the life of Jesus and how he overcame temptation to sin? (See Matt 4:1–11.)

VOCABULARY

ἀγαπᾶτε, pres. impv. act. 2d pl. of ἀγαπάω, *[do not] love*

ἀγαπᾷ, pres. subj. act. 3d sg. of ἀγαπάω, *[if anyone] loves*

ἐπιθυμία, -ας, ἡ, *lust, longing, strong desire.* The term usually carries a negative connotation in the New Testament.

σαρκός, 3d decl. fem. gen. sg. of σάρξ, *of [the] flesh*

ἀλαζονεία, -ας, ἡ, *boastfulness, vain display, pretension, arrogance*

βίος, -ου, ὁ, *life, means of living, property,* possessions. This is the word from which the terms "biology" and "biography" are derived.

ποιῶν, pres. ptcp. act. masc. nom. sg. of ποιέω, *[the one who] does*

θέλημα, θελήματος, τό, *will, wish, desire*

αἰῶνα, 3d decl. masc. acc. sg. of αἰών, αἰῶνος, *age.* εἰς τὸν αἰῶνα is an idiom meaning *forever.*

QUESTIONS

1. According to Fanning, the present tense prohibition tends to be used for "attitudes and conduct" while the aorist subjunctive prohibition is usually used for "specific commands" (*Verbal Aspect,* 327; see also Mounce, *Basics,* §33.16). Which of these categories does the prohibition in v. 15 come under? Does Fanning's theory hold true in this instance in regard to the tense of the verb?

2. How does τά function in v. 15? (See Young, *Intermediate NT Greek*, 60; Brooks and Winbery, *Syntax*, 79.)

3. According to John 3:16, God loved τὸν κόσμον. In what sense then is John using κόσμον in 1 John 2:15? (See *TDNT* 3:895.)

4. What distinct nuance is conveyed in John's use of ἀλαζονεία (v. 16) that is different from the classical and profane use of the term? (See Spicq, *Theological Lexicon*, 1:63–65.)

5. Contrast βίος (v. 16) with ζωή. (See Trench, *Synonyms*, 91–95.)

6. According to Zerwick and Grosvenor (*Grammatical Analysis*, 728), what kind of genitive is σαρκός in v. 16? (See also Hewett, *Grammar*, 198; Moule, *Idiom Book*, 39–40. For the distinction between the subjective and objective genitive, see Dana and Mantey, *Manual Grammar*, §90.5.) How are the genitives ὀφθαλμῶν and βίου used?

7. Is αὐτοῦ in v. 17 a subjective or objective genitive? Can both ideas be present in this instance? (See Smalley, *1, 2, 3 John*, 87.)

For Further Study

1. Look up the words "Monothelite" and "sarcophagus" in an unabridged English dictionary, noting both their etymology and their meaning. Identify the Greek word in vv. 15–17 from which each derives.

2. Based on your study of vv. 15–17, what is a biblical definition of "worldliness"? How might this designation apply to current times as the church seeks to identify worldliness and warn believers against it? Be sure to work issues such as materialism, secularism, security, success, and hedonism into your discussion.

3. What is the meaning of σάρξ, "flesh" in v. 16? How might Paul's contrast in Romans 7:14 between the one who is σάρκινος ("fleshly, carnal") and the law as πνευματικός ("spiritual") shed light on 1 John 2:16? Discuss.

4. What parallels exist between v. 16 and the account in Gen 3:6 of the temptation of Eve? Do you think that John is alluding to that account?

Antichrists: Sign of the Last Hour
1 John 2:18–21

VOCABULARY

ἀντίχριστος, -ου, ὁ, *Antichrist*. The term only occurs in 1 John 2:18, 22; 4:3; 2 John 7. See *TDNT* 9:571–72.

γεγόνασιν, perf. indic. act. 3d pl. of γίνομαι, *they have appeared, arisen, come on the scene*

ὅθεν, adv., *whence, wherefore, from where*

μεμενήκεισαν, pluperf. indic. act. 3d pl. of μένω, *they [would] have remained*

ἄν, untranslatable particle indicating contingency; see Mounce, *Basics*, 90.

φανερωθῶσιν, aor. subj. pass. 3d pl. of φανερόω, *they might appear, become manifest*

χρῖσμα, χρίσματος, τό, *anointment, anointing*, from χρίω, "to anoint," perhaps suggested by ἀντίχριστος in v. 18. Christians (Greek Χριστιανοί, cf. Acts 11:16) are "anointed ones" by reason of the fact that they are followers of the Anointed One and have come to know the Spirit's anointing (cf. Ps 105:15).

οἴδατε, 2d perf. indic. act. 2d pl. of οἶδα, *you know*

ψεῦδος, 3d decl. neut. nom. sg. of ψεῦδος, ψεύδους, *lie, falsehood*

QUESTIONS

1. What is the significance of the lack of an article with ἐσχάτη ὥρα in v. 18? (See Schnackenburg, *Epistles*, 132.)

_____

_____

_____

2. What kind of condition is the statement, εἰ γὰρ ἐξ ἡμῶν ἦσαν, μεμενήκεισαν ἂν μεθ' ἡμῶν (v. 19)? (See Wallace, *Grammar*, 694–96.) What assumption underlies this particular class of condition? What does the pluperfect μεμενήκεισαν express in this statement? (See Moulton, *Prolegomena*, 148.)

---

3. What do the second, third, and fourth uses of ἐξ in v. 19 connote? (See Zerwick, *Biblical Greek*, §134.)

---

4. Verse 19 contains an ellipsis (something omitted that must be provided from the context). What verbal expression from the beginning of the verse needs to be supplied between ἀλλ' and ἵνα near the end of the verse to make the thought complete? (For more ellipses in Johannine literature, see John 1:8, 31; 9:3; 13:18; 15:25.)

---

5. What effect does John's use of the emphatic ὑμεῖς in v. 20 have in relation to the apostates of v. 19? (See also ὑμεῖς in 1 John 2:24, 27; 4:4.)

---

6. How many times does the word χρῖσμα occur in the New Testament and in the Johannine epistles? (See Kubo, *Reader's Greek-English Lexicon*, 254.) What is the meaning of χρῖσμα in 2:20 and 2:27? (See *TDNT* 9:572; Stott, *Letters*, 114–15.)

---

7. In v. 20 there is a textual uncertainty. According to the textual apparatus at the bottom of the page of *GNT* and NA²⁷, some manuscripts read πάντες while others read πάντα. How is the meaning affected by these readings? Which reading is more likely to be the original? (See Metzger, *Textual Commentary*, 641.)

_____

_____

8. Occasionally a second aorist verbal form may acquire a first aorist ending. What verb in vv. 18–21 fits this description?

_____

_____

For Further Study

1. The phrase ἐσχάτη ὥρα is found only in 1 John 2:18, though John uses the word ὥρα elsewhere. What is its context and meaning? (See Robertson, *Epistles*, 215.) Compare also 2 Tim 3:1 and Heb 1:2 for two additional New Testament uses of ἔσχατος.

_____

_____

2. Does the term ἀντίχριστος (v. 18) refer to one who claims to be the χριστός or to one who opposes him? (See Trench, *Synonyms*, 105–9; cf. also Robertson, *Grammar*, 572–74, on the use of ἀντί.) What bearing might 1 John 2:22–23 and 2 John 7 have on your answer?

_____

_____

3. In an unabridged English dictionary check the etymology and meaning of the following words: eschatology, hour, horoscope, polloi (hoi polloi). Identify the Greek words in vv. 18–21 from which these words derive.

_____

_____

Who Is the Liar?
1 John 2:22–25

VOCABULARY

τίς, indef. interrog. pron. masc. nom. sg. of τίς, τί, *who? which? what?*
Note how the accent distinguishes the interrogative from the
simple indefinite pronoun, τις (cf. 1 John 2:1).

εἰ μή, *if not, except*

ἀρνούμενος, pres. ptcp. mid. masc. nom. sg. of ἀρνέομαι, *[the one
who] denies, disowns, renounces*

ὁμολογῶν, pres. ptcp. act. masc. nom. sg. of ὁμολογέω, *[the one who]
confesses*

μενέτω, pres. impv. act. 3d sg. of μένω, *let it remain, abide*

μείνῃ, aor. subj. act. 3d sg. of μένω, *[if] it remains, abides*

πατρί, 3d decl. masc. dat. sg. of πατήρ, πατρός, *father*

ἐπηγγείλατο, aor. indic. mid. 3d sg. of ἐπαγγέλλομαι, *he promised*

QUESTIONS

1. In v. 22 what exactly is the liar denying? How is the double negative
μὴ . . . οὐκ to be explained? (See Zerwick and Grosvenor, *Grammatical
Analysis*, 729; Robertson, *Grammar*, 1164; BDF §429; Young, *Intermediate NT Greek*, 203.)

_____

_____

_____

2. In v. 21 πᾶν . . . οὐκ, and in v. 23 πᾶς . . . οὐδέ may be rendered simply, "no," i.e., "*no* lie is of the truth . . . *no* one who denies the Son has the Father" (See also 1 John 3:15; 4:3.) According to Moule (*Idiom Book*, 182), what may have influenced the Greek idiom here? (See also Turner, *Syntax*, 196.)

---

3. What is the significance of the placement of ὑμεῖς at the beginning of v. 24? (See Robertson, *Epistles*, 217; BDF §466.1.)

---

4. What type of condition is expressed in v. 24? (See Brooks and Winbery, *Syntax*, 183.) What does it imply?

---

5. What added meaning does αὐτός give to v. 25? (See Grayston, *Epistles*, 91–92.)

---

6. Why in v. 25 is τὴν ζωὴν τὴν αἰώνιον in the accusative case while its antecedent (ἐπαγγελία) is nominative? (See Robertson, *Grammar*, 416.)

FOR FURTHER STUDY

1. Examine Smalley's discussion (*1, 2, 3 John*, 111–14) of the possible nature of the heresy that John addresses in v. 22.

2. What does it mean in v. 23 to "have the Father?" (See *TDNT* 2:822–24 for the Jewish background of this idea of "having God.")

3. What light may Rev 22:15 shed on the severity of John's argument about lying and liars (vv. 21–25)?

4. Does v. 24 teach that a person who does not remain constant in belief may lose his or her salvation? Discuss this Johannine passage in relation to John 15:1–8 and the totality of Scripture.

The Holy Spirit, the Internal Teacher
1 John 2:26–29

Vocabulary

πλανώντων, pres. ptcp. act. masc. gen. pl. of πλανάω, *[the ones who]*
deceive, lead astray

χρεία, -ας, ἡ, *need, necessity*

διδάσκη, pres. subj. act. 3d sg. of διδάσκω, *[that any one] should teach*

φανερωθῇ, aor. subj. pass. 3d sg. of φανερόω, *[if] he appears, is*
manifested

σχῶμεν, 2d aor. subj. act. 1st pl. of ἔχω, *we might have*

παρρησία, -ας, ἡ, *boldness, openness.* For a study of this word, see
NIDNTT 2:734–37; *TDNT* 5:871–86.

αἰσχυνθῶμεν, aor. subj. pass. 1st pl. of αἰσχύνω, *we might [not] be*
ashamed, put to shame. It is the opposite of παρρησία; not just
embarrassment, but guilt and conviction. (See Schnackenburg,
Epistles, 153.)

παρουσία, -ας, ἡ, *presence, coming, arrival.* The word does not occur
elsewhere in John, nor does he use ἐπιφάνεια, another term for
Christ's second coming. (For a study of παρουσία, see Spicq,
Theological Lexicon 3:53–55.)

εἰδῆτε, 2d perf. subj. act. 2d pl. of οἶδα, *[if] you know*

γεγέννηται, perf. indic. pass. 3d sg. of γεννάω, *he has been born,*
begotten

Questions

1. Zerwick and Grosvenor identify the participle πλανώντων in v. 26 as a conative (*Grammatical Analysis*, 729). What idea is expressed by a conative verb? (See Vaughan and Gideon, *Grammar*, 138; Brooks and Winbery, *Syntax*, 86.)

2. What is the relation of the phrase ἵνα τις διδάσκη ὑμᾶς to χρείαν in v. 27? How is the phrase being used? (See Wallace, *Grammar*, 476.) How does this use of ἵνα differ from the appositional use as seen in 1 John 3:11? (See Wallace, *Grammar*, 475.)

3. Mounce (*Lexicon*, 314) identifies μένετε in 1 John 2:27 as a second person plural present indicative active. How else could it be parsed? What do you think is the mood of μένετε in vv. 27, 28? How does the context help determine the answer?

4. Does the condition in v. 28 imply doubt as to Christ's return? (See Smith, *Epistles of John*, 182.)

5. Using Hatch and Redpath's *Concordance to the Septuagint,* find the three places in the LXX where the verb αἰσχύνω and the preposition ἀπό occur together as they do in v. 28.

6. What is the fundamental idea expressed by the use of ἀπό with αἰσχύνω in v. 28? (See Vincent, *Writings of John,* 342.)

7. What two words in v. 28 sound similar when pronounced aloud? How does this poetic touch add to the point John is making?

8. According to Turner (*Style,* 136), what style is evident in John's positioning of the attributive πᾶς before the participle (v. 29)?

For Further Study

1. According to v. 27 every Christian has the "anointing" of the Holy Spirit. He lives within (cf. Rom 8:9) and provides illumination of God's word. At the same time, every Christian has a conscience (cf. 2 Cor 1:12). Is there a difference between a believer's conscience and the Holy Spirit? Should a Christian accept the popular saying, "Let your conscience be your guide"? Discuss.

2. In v. 27 John seems to be saying that if you have the Holy Spirit as your (internal) teacher and guide to truth (cf. John 14:7; 16:13), human teachers are unnecessary; you are to depend on the Spirit to teach you all things. Do you agree? Discuss v. 27 in light of the historical background of 1 John and the totality of New Testament thought.

3. To "abide" or "remain" in Christ (vv. 27–28) is spiritual or mystical language. Johannine literature is characterized by this kind of abstract thought. How would you explain to another Christian what John means by "abiding" in Christ?

4. How does the tense of ποιῶν (v. 29) affect our idea of Christian living?

God's Children: Now and in the Future
1 John 3:1–3

VOCABULARY

ἴδετε, 2d aor. impv. act. 2d pl. of ὁράω, *behold, see, look*. The verb conveys a sense of urgency here. See Schnackenburg, *Epistles*, 155.

ποταπός, -ή, -όν, *what? of what sort? what kind of?*

δέδωκεν, perf. indic. act. 3d sg. of δίδωμι, *he has given*

κληθῶμεν, aor. subj. pass. 1st pl. of καλέω, *[that] we should be called, named*. This is probably an example of a divine or theological passive as in Matt 5:9. For the meaning of this idiom, see Zerwick, *Biblical Greek*, §236; Wallace, *Grammar*, 437–38.

ἔγνω, 2d aor. indic. act. 3d sg. of γινώσκω, *it has [not] known, perceived, understood*

οὔπω, adv., *not yet*

ἐσόμεθα, fut. indic. mid. 1st pl. of εἰμί, *we will be*

οἴδαμεν, 2d perf. indic. act. 1st pl. of οἶδα, *we know*

ὅμοιος, -α, -ον, *like, similar to*

ὀψόμεθα, fut. indic. mid. 1st pl. of ὁράω, *we shall see*

ἁγνίζω, *purify*. In the New Testament the word often carries an ethical sense. See Schnackenburg, *Epistles*, 161; *TDNT* 1:123. The -ιζω suffix conveys a causal idea. See Chamberlain, *Exegetical Grammar*, 15.

ἁγνός, -ή, -όν, *pure, clean, holy*. See Trench, *Synonyms*, 331–34.

QUESTIONS

1. What was the original definition of ποταπός (v. 1)? (See Zerwick and Grosvenor, *Grammatical Analysis*, 729.) What effect does this original meaning have when applied to v. 1? (See Chamberlain, *Exegetical Grammar*, 52; Spicq, *Theological Lexicon* 3:143–44.)

2. What does the tense of δέδωκεν (v. 1) suggest regarding God's love for his adopted children?

3. How does the ἵνα clause function in v. 1? (See Chamberlain, *Exegetical Grammar*, 185–86; Burton, *Syntax*, §213.)

4. What is the subject of ἐφανερώθη in v. 2? (See Brown, *Epistles*, 394.) Why does John use the neuter τί rather than the masculine form τίς? (See Robertson, *Epistles*, 220.)

5. What four meanings of ὅμοιος (v. 2) are to be distinguished in classical usage? (See *NIDNTT* 2:500–501.) The same volume notes, concerning Christ, that at present we have only a "token knowledge of his true being." On the other hand, at the return of Christ, a different kind of relationship will be possible. How is this new relationship described in connection with 1 John 3:2? (See *NIDNTT* 2:503.)

6. Look up ἐπί in BAGD. Which definition applies in v. 3?

7. What is the antecedent of τὴν ἐλπίδα ταύτην (v. 3)? What, according to v. 3, is the practical outcome of this expectation? What, therefore, should be the ultimate result of the study of end times (eschatology)?

FOR FURTHER STUDY

1. Utilizing Greenlee, become acquainted with the general principles and rules used by textual critics in their attempt to determine the original reading when faced with a textual variant (*Textual Criticism*, 111–16). Examine Greenlee's discussion of the textual variants in 1 John 3:1 (*Textual Criticism*, 124–25). Which reading appears to be the original: the inclusion of καὶ ἐσμέν, or the omission of the words? Explain your answer.

2. The expression "children of God," or "sons of God," is used in a variety of ways in Scripture. For example, compare the meaning of the term "sons of God" in Gen 6:2 and Job 1:6 with the expression "children of God" in 1 John 3:1–2. The meaning of a biblical expression is determined not by dictionary definitions or by etymology, but by context. How does the general context of 1 John and other Johannine literature (e.g., John 1:12) help us find the meaning of "children of God" in 1 John 3:1–2?

3. Does v. 1 support the view that God is the Father of all people, or does this text teach that God is only the Father of some people? Discuss the biblical concept of the fatherhood of God (cf. Mal 2:10). Work into your discussion John 1:12 and the New Testament terms "adoption" and "Abba" (see Rom 8:14–16).

4. Christians sometimes say or sing that they want to "be like Jesus." In light of your study of this passage (especially v. 2), what do you think it will mean for Christians to become "like Jesus" at his appearing?

A Contrast: The Sinful and the Righteous
1 John 3:4–8

VOCABULARY

ἀνομία, -ας, ἡ, *lawlessness, transgression.* The α- prefix (an alpha privative) negates the word to which it is attached, "that which is without the law (*νόμος*)." See also ἀδικίας in 1:9.

ἄρῃ, aor. subj. act. 3d sg. of αἴρω, *[that] he might take away.* See John 1:29.

μένων, pres. ptcp. act. masc. nom. sg. of μένω, *[the one who] remains, abides*

ἁμαρτάνων, pres. ptcp. act. masc. nom. sg. of ἁμαρτάνω, *[the one who] sins*

ἑώρακεν, perf. indic. act. 3d sg. of ὁράω, *he has [not] seen*

ἔγνωκεν, perf. indic. act. 3d sg. of γινώσκω, *he has come to know*

πλανάτω, pres. impv. act. 3d sg. of πλανάω, *let [no one] mislead, deceive*

διάβολος, -ου, ὁ, *devil, slanderer.* From the verb διαβάλλω, *accuse, bring charges with hostile intent.*

λύσῃ, aor. subj. act. 3d sg. of λύω, *[that] he might undo, destroy.* The word suggests here destruction by undoing that which forms the bond of cohesion. See Rogers and Rogers, *New Linguistic and Exegetical Key*, 596.

QUESTIONS

1. How does John's emphasis on sin in 3:4–10 differ from that in 1:7–2:2? (See Johnson, *1, 2, and 3 John*, 69.)

2. What is the distinction in meaning between ἡ ἁμαρτία and ἡ ἀνομία (v. 4)? (See Trench, *Synonyms*, 239–44.) What grammatical inference can be drawn from the fact that the article occurs with both nouns? (See Robertson, *Grammar*, 767–68.)

3. Using *TDNT* 1:185–86, make a brief study of the origin and meaning of αἴρω (v. 5).

4. Give an expanded translation of v. 6, emphasizing the significance of the verbal tenses.

5. The word ποιέω occurs four times in vv. 4–8. How many times is the verb found in 1 John? (See Kohlenberger, Goodrick, and Swanson, *Exhaustive Concordance*.) What does this indicate regarding the importance of "doing"?

6. Does ἐκεῖνος (vv. 5, 7) always refer to Christ in 1 John? (See Kohlenberger, Goodrick, and Swanson, *Exhaustive Concordance*.) What is the significance of John's use of the term? (See Vincent, *Writings of John*, 61.)

7. The verb ἁμαρτάνει (v. 8) is a progressive present of duration (also known as a present of past action still in progress). It is to be translated "has been sinning." Study this use of the present tense in Burton (*Syntax*, §17) and Wallace (*Grammar*, 519–20). Why does John use the present tense with regard to the devil rather than the aorist or imperfect? (See Vincent, *Writings of John*, 348.) What is significant about the fact that the same tense is used earlier in v. 8 of the one who "practices sin"?

8. What does John have in mind when he refers in v. 8 to the fact that the devil has been sinning ἀπ᾽ ἀρχῆς? Is this a reference to the beginning of his existence or to the beginning of human history, i.e., Adam and Eve's fall (Gen 3:1–7)? (Consult the commentaries for assistance.)

For Further Study

1. The words "atheist," "apathetic," "agnostic," and "apolitical" are words derived from Greek roots to which the alpha privative has been prefixed (see ἀνομία in the vocabulary for this assignment). What other English words using an alpha privative can you add to the above list?

2. Read Psalm 1. How does it provide a broad theological foundation for John's argument in 1 John 3:4–8?

3. For John, the devil is the dominant reality behind all sin (v. 8). Compare and contrast John's description of the devil with popular current views. What other relevant Scriptures can you bring into the discussion?

_____

_____

_____

_____

Children of God and Children of the Devil
1 John 3:9–12

Vocabulary

γεγεννημένος, perf. ptcp. pass. masc. nom. sg. of γεννάω, *[the one who has been] born, begotten*

σπέρμα, σπέρματος, τό, *seed, offspring, posterity*

δύναμαι, *be able*

ἁμαρτάνειν, pres. infin. act. of ἁμαρτάνω, *to sin*

φανερός, -ά, -όν, *visible, clear, plainly to be seen, manifest, known.* See Moulton and Milligan, *Vocabulary of the Greek Testament*, 663.

ἀγαπῶμεν, pres. subj. act. 1st pl. of ἀγαπάω, *[that] we might love*

Κάϊν, indeclinable, *Cain*

σφάζω, *slay, slaughter, murder,* literally *to cut the throat.* See Vincent, *Writings of John*, 350, for references to the use of the word in the *Iliad* and *Odyssey;* for other references in classical literature, see Liddell and Scott, *Greek-English Lexicon*, 1737–38.

χάριν, prep. with gen., *for, on account of, for the sake of, because of.* Here it functions in a question, *on what account? why?*

Questions

1. Does v. 9 teach sinless perfection? Give particular attention to the tense of ποιεῖ and ἁμαρτάνειν. (For an examination of the question of 1 John 3:6–9 and sinless perfection, see Stott, *Letters*, 134–40.)

_____

_____

_____

2. 1 John 3:9 exhibits a common stylistic feature in biblical Greek, namely, chiasm. The word "chiasm" comes from the Greek letter chi (X). A chiasm is an inverted arrangement where parallel terms or phrases occur in reverse order (see *ISBE* 3:895). In the following example from Mark 2:27, note how the first and last items are parallel and the second and third are parallel:

> A The Sabbath was made
> B for man
> B′ not man
> A′ for the Sabbath

In some cases there is a center item that the parallel items move towards and away from, i.e., A B C B′ A′. This is the kind of chiastic pattern found in 1 John 3:9. See if you can identify the items in the verse that make up this structure.

---

3. What is significant in v. 10 about the adjective-article-noun position of φανερά . . . τὰ τέκνα? (See Wallace, *Grammar*, 307–8.)

---

4. What does the punctuation mark mean after the word διαβόλου in the middle of v. 10? (See Mounce, *Basics*, 14.)

---

5. In v. 11 which word is the subject, αὕτη or ἡ ἀγγελία (cf. 1 John 5:9)? Why? (See Wallace, *Grammar*, 43–44.)

---

6. What is the origin of the word χάριν in v. 12? (See Moule, *Idiom Book*, 86.)

7. In v. 12 what are the two dots used in the name Κάϊν called and what do they indicate? (See also Ἀλληλουϊά in Rev 19:1, 3, 4, 6. See Mounce, *Basics*, §3.5; Robertson, *Grammar*, 204–5.)

For Further Study

1. How does Zerwick (*Biblical Greek*, §251) resolve the paradox of 1 John 2:1 and 1 John 3:9, in which John assumes that Christians can sin then later appears to teach that they cannot?

2. The term σπέρμα (v. 9) appears to be a metaphor for something God shares with each of his spiritual children, i.e., believers. In the context of 1 John and the rest of Scripture, what are some of the possible ways to interpret this word picture?

3. Check the LXX rendering of Gen 4:8 in Rahlfs' *Septuaginta*. Is the verb σφάζω used for the action of Cain against his brother (cf. 1 John 3:12)? Discuss how the use of the Hebrew and Greek texts of the Old Testament by the writers of the New Testament relates to questions of inspiration, infallibility, and inerrancy. Did the New Testament writers use the Old Testament word-for-word or idea-for-idea?

4. The word σφάζω, introduced in this lesson, may be onomatopoetic. What is onomatopoeia (consult an English dictionary), and how may it apply to the sound of σφάζω? As another New Testament example of an onomatopoetic verb, pronounce the verb πτύω, and then look up its meaning in BAGD.

Love and Hate
1 John 3:13–15

Vocabulary

θαυμάζετε, pres. impv. act. 2d pl. of θαυμάζω, *[do not] marvel,
wonder, be amazed*

μεταβεβήκαμεν, perf. indic. act. 1st pl. of μεταβαίνω, *we have passed
over, moved* (from one place to another). See *TDNT* 1:523.

ἀνθρωποκτόνος, -ου, ὁ, *murderer* (ἄνθρωπος + κτείνω, "man killer")

μένουσαν, pres. ptcp. act. fem. acc. sg. of μένω, *abiding, remaining*

Questions

1. Sometimes μή with a present imperative calls for the cessation of an
   activity already in progress. (See Wallace, *Grammar*, 724; note, however, his caution, 714–17.) Do you think that John is assuming in
   v. 13 that these Christians were in fact already marveling? If so, how
   would you paraphrase the prohibition?

2. Why does John depart from his normal custom of addressing his readers as "beloved" (2:7; 3:2; 4:1, 7, 11) or "children" (2:1; 2:12, 14, 18, 28;
   3:7, 18; 4:4; 5:21) and address them as ἀδελφοί in v. 13? (The term
   occurs nowhere else in Johannine literature as a direct form of address.) Examine the immediate context.

3. What idea is conveyed by εἰ in v. 13? (See Burton, *Syntax*, §277; Young, *Intermediate NT Greek*, 185.)

4. How do the tense of μεταβεβήκαμεν and that of ἀγαπῶμεν highlight John's argument in v. 14? (See Schnackenburg, *Epistles*, 180.)

5. What is the significance of the definite article with θάνατος and ζωή in v. 14? (See Vincent, *Writings of John*, 350.)

6. How common is the noun ἀνθρωποκτόνος (v. 15) in ancient literature? (See BAGD.) How many times is this word used in the New Testament? Where? How may this information be helpful in assessing the question of the authorship of 1 John?

7. How is the participle μένουσαν (v. 15) functioning syntactically? Is it being used substantivally, adjectivally, or adverbially? Why? (See Greenlee, *Exegetical Grammar*, 56; Wallace, *Grammar*, 618–19.)

FOR FURTHER STUDY

1. Apart from verse 12, the New Testament mentions Cain by name only in Heb 11:4. What does that text say about the sacrifice offered God by Cain's brother Abel? What Greek word found in 1 John 3:12 and Heb 11:4 describes the actions or character of Abel in comparison to Cain? Finally, according to Heb 12:24, why is the blood of Jesus said to "speak better" (i.e., "it speaks more graciously") than the blood of Abel shed by Cain?

2. Based upon v. 15b some believe that homicide is an unforgivable sin. Evaluate this interpretation of v. 15b in the light of v. 15a.

3. How is Jesus' Sermon on the Mount (note especially Matt 5:21–24; 43–48) useful in understanding John's teaching in v. 15 that hatred of one's brother qualifies one as an ἀνθρωποκτόνος, a "murderer"?

Proof of Real Love
1 John 3:16–20

VOCABULARY

ἔθηκεν, aor. indic. act. 3d sg. of τίθημι, *he laid down [his life]*. See
John 10:11, 17–18.

θεῖναι, 2d aor. infin. act. of τίθημι, *to lay down*

ἔχῃ, pres. subj. act. 3d sg. of ἔχω, *[whoever] has*

θεωρῇ, pres. subj. act. 3d sg. of θεωρέω, *[whoever] sees, observes, looks
at*. This is the only occurrence of the verb in 1 John. See Vincent,
Writings of John, 59. Note that the English words "theory" and
"theorem" derive from this root.

ἔχοντα, pres. ptcp. act. masc. acc. sg. of ἔχω, *having*

κλείσῃ, aor. subj. act. 3d sg. of κλείω, *[whoever] closes, shuts*

σπλάγχνα, pl. of σπλάγχνον, -ου, τό, *inward parts, entrails, heart,
affections, the seat of emotions*

πῶς, adv., *how?*

γλῶσσα, -ης, ἡ, *tongue, speech*. The English words "glossary," "glosso-
lalia," and "polyglot" are derived from γλῶσσα.

ἔμπροσθεν, prep. with gen., *in front of, before*

πείθω, *persuade, reassure*

καταγινώσκῃ, pres. subj. act. 3d sg. of καταγινώσκω, takes the genitive, *[in whatever our heart] condemns*. Note the play on words in
v. 20 between καταγινώσκω and γινώσκω

μείζων (masc. nom. sg. of the 3d decl. adj. μείζων, μεῖζον), *greater*

QUESTIONS

1. Which words are emphasized in v. 16? (See question 2 in the FOR FURTHER STUDY section of ASSIGNMENT 1.)

2. Study the meaning of ὑπέρ with the genitive in *NIDNTT* 3:1196–97. What fundamental idea is inherent in this construction? Is Christ in v. 16 being depicted as a representative, a substitute, as both, or as neither? Support your answer from the context and Johannine parallels (John 10:11, 15; 11:50–52; 18:14).

3. In v. 17 the NIV translates σπλάγχνα "pity." Show how context affects the literal or figurative use of this word throughout the New Testament. (See *TDNT* 7:553–57.)

4. According to Westcott (*Epistles of John*, 115), what is the function of the datives λόγῳ, γλώσσῃ, ἔργῳ, and ἀληθείᾳ in v. 18?

5. Verse 19 contains two of the only eight occurrences of the future tense in 1 John. Why does John use the future here and not the present tense? To what future situation is he referring? (See Smalley, *1, 2, 3 John*, 201; Marshall, *Epistles*, 197.)

6. In v. 20, how should ὅτι ἐάν be taken? (See Marshall, *Epistles*, 197 n. 4.) What is the difference in meaning between ὅτι ἐάν and ὅ τι ἐάν?

7. What is the meaning of the word καρδία in vv. 19–21? (See *EDNT* 2:250.1.) How is the genitive τῆς καρδίας used in v. 20? (See Dana and Mantey, *Manual Grammar*, §91.4.) Why does John use the singular τῆς καρδίας when the word is modified by the plural ἡμῶν? (See Turner, *Syntax*, 23.)

8. Is God's greatness in v. 20 to be related to his judgment (i.e., if our heart condemns us, how much more will God) or to his mercy (i.e., if our heart condemns us, how much more will God be compassionate)?

FOR FURTHER STUDY

1. In v. 16, the exhortation ἡμεῖς ὀφείλομεν ὑπὲρ τῶν ἀδελφῶν τὰς ψυχὰς θεῖναι is "tough theology" for any Christian. What do you think this meant in the early church, and what does it mean (in practical terms) today?

2. According to Acts 2:44–45, the Jerusalem church "had everything in common" and "they gave to anyone as he had need." The Greek idiom, χρείαν ἔχειν, "to have need" is reflected in both Acts 2:45 and 1 John 3:17. What is the difference between a "need" and a "want"? Is this radical kind of Christian commitment to provide for the needs of one's brother (cf. Jas 2:14–17) an obligation for all Christians in this modern world or only for some? Discuss.

3. Bultmann argues that the phrase ἔμπροσθεν αὐτοῦ in v. 19 has a judicial connotation (*Epistles*, 56 n. 59). Does the context support this interpretation? If so, in what sense would God be depicted? How would the Christian be depicted? Paraphrase vv. 19–20 from this perspective.

Confidence before God
1 John 3:21–24

VOCABULARY

αἰτῶμεν, pres. subj. act. 1st pl. of αἰτέω, *[whatever] we ask*
ἀρεστός, -ή, -όν, *pleasing, agreeable, acceptable*
ἐνώπιον, prep. with gen., *before, in the presence of*
πιστεύσωμεν, aor. subj. act. 1st pl. of πιστεύω, *[that] we believe*
ἔδωκεν, aor. indic. act. 3d sg. of δίδωμι, *he gave*
πνεῦμα, πνεύματος, τό, *Spirit.* This is the first occurrence of the word
   in 1 John.

QUESTIONS

1. Why does καρδία precede the verb καταγινώσκη in v. 21 when in
   v. 20 it follows the verb? (See question 2 in the FOR FURTHER STUDY
   section of ASSIGNMENT 1.)

2. What two preconditions does John give in v. 22 for answered prayer?
   What does the tense of τηροῦμεν and ποιοῦμεν imply in this regard?

3. How is the phrase ἐνώπιον αὐτοῦ in v. 22 to be understood? (See BDF §214.6.)

4. Identify the type of ἵνα clause used in v. 23 (cf. 1 John 3:11). (See Wallace, *Grammar*, 475–76.)

5. Brown notes that the use of the various forms of αὐτός in the clause καὶ ὁ τηρῶν τὰς ἐντολὰς αὐτοῦ ἐν αὐτῷ μένει καὶ αὐτὸς ἐν αὐτῷ (v. 24) is an example of a rhetorical device known as paronomasia (*Epistles*, 464). What exactly is paronomasia? (See Robertson, *Short Grammar*, §474.q.)

6. How does the preposition ἐκ function in v. 24? (For options see Brooks and Winbery, *Syntax*, 65.)

7. If οὗ is the object of the verb ἔδωκεν in v. 24, why is it in the genitive case rather than the accusative? (See Rogers and Rogers, *New Linguistic and Exegetical Key*, 597; Wallace, *Grammar*, 338–39; Zerwick, *Biblical Greek*, §16–21; Mounce, *Basics*, §14.15.)

FOR FURTHER STUDY

1. The first part of 1 John 3:22 ("we receive from him [God] whatever we ask") has sometimes been read as suggesting that Christians may expect to get anything they want from God. Assess this interpretation in the light of the whole of 1 John and of Scripture. Broaden your discussion to include the (correct) use and abuse of "proof texts" in general.

2. The word ἐντολή, "commandment," occurs four times in vv. 22–24. Clearly, this passage teaches that Christians are expected to keep God's commandments; they are not optional. Indeed, Paul says the ἐντολή of God is "holy, righteous, and good" (Rom 7:12). But to which group of ἐντολαί does 1 John 3:22–24 refer? Every teaching of the Bible? The 613 commandments of the law of Moses? The moral law or the Ten Commandments? Only two commandments: to love God and to love your neighbor as yourself? Discuss.

3. How is the dative τῷ ὀνόματι being used in v. 23? (See Wallace, *Grammar*, 171–73.) Does there appear to be a difference in meaning between πιστεύω with the dative and πιστεύω εἰς with the accusative τὸ ὄνομα (cf. 1 John 5:13; John 1:12; 2:23; 3:18)? (See Schnackenburg, *Epistles*, 189.) What is meant by believing and praying in Jesus' name? Discuss.

Test the Spirits
1 John 4:1–3

VOCABULARY

πιστεύετε, pres. impv. act. 2d pl. of πιστεύω, *[do not] believe*
δοκιμάζετε, pres. impv. act. 2d pl. of δοκιμάζω, *test, examine, prove, approve*
ψευδοπροφήτης, -ου, ὁ, *false prophet*
ἐξεληλύθασιν, 2d perf. indic. act. 3d pl. of ἔρχομαι, *they have gone out*
ἐληλυθότα, 2d perf. ptcp. act. masc. acc. sg. of ἔρχομαι, *having come*
ἀκηκόατε, 2d perf. indic. act. 2d pl. of ἀκούω, *you have heard*

QUESTIONS

1. Why do you think that John used ἀλλά instead of δέ in v. 1? (See BDF §448.1.)

2. What does πνεῦμα mean in v. 1? (See *NIDNTT* 3:695; BAGD, s.v. πνεῦμα 7.)

3. What is the special use and translation of εἰ in v. 1? (See BAGD, s.v. εἰ V.2.)

4. What does the tense of ἐξεληλύθασιν (v. 1) convey in regard to the coming of false prophets?

5. How does the participle ἐληλυθότα function in v. 2? (See Wallace, *Grammar*, 645–46; note how Brooks and Winbery [*Syntax*, 150–51] categorize this usage.)

6. What does the tense of ἐληλυθότα (v. 2) imply regarding the Christian view of the incarnation? (See Stott, *Letters*, 157–58.) In what way is v. 2 a further commentary upon the opening theme of John's letter (1:1–4)?

7. What word would naturally be provided to agree with the article τό before τοῦ ἀντιχρίστου in v. 3? How is this τό being used? (See Wallace, *Grammar*, 235–36.)

8. What is the significance of ἤδη at the end of the final clause of v. 3 and of νῦν at its beginning? (See Smalley, *1, 2, 3 John*, 225.)

FOR FURTHER STUDY

1. In v. 1 John warns against ψευδοπροφῆται, "false prophets," a theme common to both Old and New Testaments. What characteristics distinguish a false prophet from a true prophet of God? (See Deut 13:1–5; 18:20–22; Gal 1:6–9.)

2. One of the most common verbs of theological significance in Johannine literature is πιστεύω. Accordingly, a term John employs frequently for a Christian is ὁ πιστεύων, "the one who believes" (1 John 5:1, 10; etc.). In 4:1, however, John cautions the church about believing everything and everyone. When should Christians, whether in John's day or today, be skeptical rather than naively trusting? Are the first two verbs in 4:1 singular or plural? How might the answer to this question be a clue to one of the ways spirits not of God can be detected?

3. According to Stott (*Letters*, 157–59), what is the meaning of the formula for testing the spirits in v. 2? What teaching was John perhaps repudiating?

How to Recognize the Two Spirits
1 John 4:4–6

VOCABULARY

ἤ, *than, or.* See Turner, *Syntax,* 216; BDF §185.2.

γινώσκων, pres. ptcp. act. masc. nom. sg. of γινώσκω, *[the one who] knows*

πλάνη, -ης, ἡ, *deceit, error, going astray, wandering.* Note πλανάω, *mislead, lead astray.*

QUESTIONS

1. What pronouns does John use in vv. 4–6 to emphasize and highlight the contrast between the Christians (or more specifically, the apostles) and the false teachers? Examine carefully the clauses in which these words occur. In what position are these pronouns placed?

2. What light do such verses as 1 John 2:29 and 3:9–10 shed on the meaning of ὑμεῖς ἐκ τοῦ θεοῦ ἐστε in v. 4?

3. What does the tense of the verb νενικήκατε (v. 4) imply regarding the victory of John's followers over the false teachers? (See Smalley, *1, 2, 3 John*, 226; Burton, *Syntax*, §74.)

_____

_____

_____

4. According to Brown (*Epistles*, 498), what idea does ἀκούω with the genitive express in v. 5?

_____

_____

_____

5. Who are the ἡμεῖς (and ἡμῶν) in v. 6? (For differing viewpoints, see Stott, *Letters*, 161–62; Brown, *Epistles*, 498–99.)

_____

_____

_____

6. How is the phrase ἐκ τούτου being used in v. 6? (See Moule, *Idiom Book*, 73.) What is the antecedent of τούτου? (See Haas, DeJonge, and Swellengrebel, *Translator's Handbook*, 105.)

_____

_____

_____

7. Does the phrase τὸ πνεῦμα τῆς ἀληθείας (v. 6) refer to the Holy Spirit? (Consult Kohlenberger, Goodrick, and Swanson's *Exhaustive Concordance* to see if this phrase occurs elsewhere in John's writings.)

_____

_____

_____

For Further Study

1. Who is ὁ ἐν τῷ κόσμῳ (v. 4)? Utilizing Kohlenberger, Goodrick, and Swanson's *Exhaustive Concordance*, substantiate your answer by examining other passages from 1 John where the term κόσμος occurs.

2. Verse 4 rules out cosmic dualism—the teaching of two equal powers vying for control with the end in doubt. Rather, John teaches that the power and presence of God resident in every believer is greater (μείζων) than that of ὁ ἐν τῷ κόσμῳ. The book of Revelation expresses the ultimate universal climax of this present reality. How might the comparative adjective μείζων (in reference to God) encourage believers serving in particularly dark and difficult places? In what tangible ways in the history of the church and in your life has God proven to be greater than "the one who is in the world"?

3. What is the Old Testament meaning behind ἀλήθεια (v. 6)? (See *TDNT* 1:232–33.) How does John use ἀλήθεια in his writings? (See *TDNT* 1:245–47.)

Demonstration of Love
1 John 4:7–10

VOCABULARY

μονογενῆ, masc. acc. sg. of the 3d decl. adj. μονογενής, -ές, *only, only begotten, unique in kind*

ἀπέσταλκεν, perf. indic. act. 3d sg. of ἀποστέλλω, *he has sent.* The perfect tense here emphasizes the continuing effect of God sending his Son.

ζήσωμεν, aor. subj. act. 1st pl. of ζάω, *[that] we might live*

ἠγαπήκαμεν, perf. indic. act. 1st pl. of ἀγαπάω, *we have loved.* The essence of love is not our love for God, however lasting (as indicated by the perfect tense) it may be (see Smalley, *1, 2, 3 John,* 243).

QUESTIONS

1. What is the significance of the mood of ἀγαπῶμεν in v. 7? (See Brooks and Winbery, *Syntax,* 118; McKay, *Syntax,* §9.2.)

2. What kind of pronoun is ἀλλήλους (v. 7), and what is its etymology? (See Robertson, *Short Grammar,* §378.)

3. In v. 8 are we free to translate ὁ θεὸς ἀγάπη ἐστίν "love is God"? Why or why not? (See Robertson, *Grammar*, 768, 794; Wallace, *Grammar*, 264.)

_____

_____

_____

4. In what position does the adjective μονογενής stand in v. 9? What does the use of this word in reference to Jesus imply? (See *TDNT* 4:740–41.)

_____

_____

_____

5. How should the phrase ἐν ἡμῖν in v. 9 be translated? (See Zerwick and Grosvenor, *Grammatical Analysis*, 731; Haas, DeJonge, and Swellengrebel, *Translator's Handbook*, 108.)

_____

_____

_____

6. How is ὅτι being used in v. 10? (See Hewett, *Grammar*, 52.) Which ὅτι clause in v. 10 is receiving the emphasis?

_____

_____

7. The nouns τὸν υἱόν and ἱλασμόν (v. 10) are functioning as double accusatives in relation to the verb ἀπέστειλεν (see 1:10; 4:14). Which noun is the object and which is the complement? (See Wallace, *Grammar*, 186.)

_____

_____

_____

For Further Study

1. Love is one of the key themes of 1 John, a theme treated with especially great intensity in 4:7–5:3. Of the first six words of this section,
   three are the forms of the word "love" that occur most frequently in
   this letter (ἀγαπητός, ἀγαπάω, ἀγάπη). John exhorts Christians—as
   Scripture does elsewhere—to imitate the character of God. But is love
   the most important of all God's attributes? Some Christians, for instance, have insisted that holiness, or justice, or mercy is equally
   important. Using vv. 7ff. as your starting point, discuss the position
   Scripture gives to ἀγάπη in comparison to the other attributes of God.

2. In vv. 7–8 John uses the word γινώσκω in regard to knowing God.
   What does it mean to "know God"? What role do intellect (the cogni-
   tive) and experience (the affective) have in relation to this question?
   Did the Semitic (Old Testament) understanding of knowledge differ from
   that found in classical Greek thought? To what source(s) should the
   Christian turn in seeking to define this important theological topic?

3. Note the order of the words in the central clause of v. 9: ὅτι τὸν υἱὸν
   αὐτοῦ τὸν μονογενῆ ἀπέσταλκεν ὁ θεὸς εἰς τὸν κόσμον. What is
   being emphasized? How does this emphasis relate to the main point of
   the verse?

Love and the Indwelling Presence of God
1 John 4:11–15

VOCABULARY

ἀγαπᾶν, pres. infin. act. of ἀγαπάω, *to love*

πώποτε, adv., *ever, at any time*

τεθέαται, perf. indic. mid. 3d sg. of θεάομαι, *[no one] has seen, beheld, looked upon*

τετελειωμένη ἐστίν, perf. periphr. indic. pass. 3d sg. of τελειόω, *it has been perfected, completed*

τεθεάμεθα, perf. indic. mid. 1st pl. of θεάομαι, *we have beheld, looked upon, seen*

σωτῆρα, 3d decl. masc. acc. sg. of σωτήρ, σωτῆρος, *savior, preserver, deliverer.* See Spicq, *Theological Lexicon* 3:351–56.

ὁμολογήσῃ, aor. subj. act. 3d sg. of ὁμολογέω, *[whoever] confesses*

QUESTIONS

1. What kind of conditional sentence is found in v. 11? (See Wallace, *Grammar*, 690–94.) What does the condition imply here?

---

2. To what does οὕτως in v. 11 refer? In what well-known verse in the third chapter of John's Gospel does this adverb occur? What parallels of thought exist between that verse and 1 John 4:7–11?

3. What might the significance be of the anarthrous accusative θεόν in v. 12 (cf. John 1:18)? (See Westcott, *Epistles*, 151; Smalley, *1, 2, 3 John*, 246.)

4. Robertson sees ἐκ τοῦ πνεύματος αὐτοῦ (v. 13) as an example of the "partitive" use of the preposition ἐκ (*Grammar*, 599). If so, how should the phrase be translated? (For a definition of the partitive ["wholative"], see Wallace, *Grammar*, 84–85.)

5. What does the tense of γινώσκομεν and μένομεν in v. 13 suggest? (See Smalley, *1, 2, 3 John*, 249.)

6. What statements from 1 John 1:2 do the perfect τεθεάμεθα and the present μαρτυροῦμεν of v. 14 echo?

7. What is the theological significance of John's emphasis in v. 15 on the human name Ἰησοῦς? (See Johnson, *1, 2, 3 John*, 111.)

8. Identify the chiastic structure in the words ὁ θεὸς ἐν αὐτῷ μένει καὶ αὐτὸς ἐν τῷ θεῷ (v. 15).

For Further Study

1. Verse 12 says that "no one has ever seen God." Yet in Matt 5:8 the Lord says the pure in heart "shall see God." Do these statements conflict?

2. The πνεῦμα of God has many functions or roles in Scripture. Verse 13 teaches that the Holy Spirit assures believers of their relation with God. What other resources besides the πνεῦμα does God provide believers to assure them of their standing? Be sure to work 1 John 3:24 into your discussion.

3. Using Kohlenberger, Goodrick, and Swanson, *Exhaustive Concordance*, locate all the instances of the verb ὁμολογέω in 1 John. What is the object of the verb in each case? What conclusions can you draw about the range of meaning of this verb in 1 John?

4. Brown states that the aorist ὁμολογήσῃ (v. 15) signifies "the single basic public confession of faith" that makes one a Christian (*Epistles*, 524). Is this "once and for all" nuance a legitimate inference from the tense, or is Brown drawing from the aorist a meaning that the tense itself does not convey? (See Carson, *Exegetical Fallacies*, 68–73.)

5. The term ὁμολογέω, which is used in v. 15, gives rise to the word "homologoumena," which is used in regard to the canon of Scripture. Check an unabridged English dictionary (or theological dictionary) for the definition of this term. How does this word contrast with the word "antilegomena"?

God's Love and Our Love
1 John 4:16–21

VOCABULARY

πεπιστεύκαμεν, perf. indic. act. 1st pl. of πιστεύω, *we have come to believe*

ἔχωμεν, pres. subj. act. 1st pl. of ἔχω, *[that] we may have*

κρίσεως, 3d decl. fem. gen. sg. of κρίσις, *judgment, decision*

τελεία, fem. nom. sg. of τέλειος, -α, -ον, *complete, perfect, mature, having attained the end or purpose.* For words formed on the root τελ- that occur frequently in the New Testament see Metzger, *Lexical Aids,* 69.

ἔξω, adv., *out, without*

κόλασιν, 3d decl. fem. acc. sg. of κόλασις, κολάσεως, *punishment, correction, penalty.* It is used only here and in Matt 25:46.

φοβούμενος, pres. ptcp. pass. masc. nom. sg. of φοβέομαι, *[the one who] fears*

εἴπῃ, 2d aor. subj. act. 3d sg. of λέγω, *[if anyone] says*

μισῇ, pres. subj. act. 3d sg. of μισέω, *[if anyone] hates*

ἀγαπᾷ, pres. subj. act. 3d sg. of ἀγαπάω, *he should love*

QUESTIONS

1. Why does πιστεύω take the accusative in v. 16 when it usually takes the dative? (See Grayston, *Epistles,* 127.)

2. What phrasing found in the ὅτι clause of v. 17 is echoed through 1 John 2:6; 3:3, 7?

3. Why does φόβος in v. 18 appear first without the article and then twice with the article? (See Grayston, *Epistles*, 131.)

4. In the phrase found in v. 18, ἡ τελεία ἀγάπη (article-adjective-noun), which word receives the greater emphasis, the adjective or the noun? (See Wallace, *Grammar*, 306.)

5. How do Zerwick and Grosvenor suggest ἔχει should be translated in v. 18? (See *Grammatical Analysis*, 732.)

6. Is the mood of ἀγαπῶμεν in v. 19 indicative (i.e., "we love") or subjunctive (i.e., "let us love")? Why?

7. In some contexts where ὅτι is found, the term is left untranslated into English. Why? Is v. 20 one of those contexts? If so, how should ὅτι be represented in v. 20? (For help in understanding ὅτι in v. 20 see Goetchius, *Language of the NT*, §321.1.c; Wenham, *Elements*, 107 [3].)

_____

_____

8. How should the second occurrence of καί in v. 21 be translated?

_____

_____

_____

For Further Study

1. Is the τελεία ἀγάπη that casts out fear (v. 18) our love for God or God's love for us? (Note the immediate context, especially vv. 12, 17 where τελειόω and ἀγάπη occur together.)

_____

_____

2. According to v. 19 what assumption underlies our love of others? (Note the causal use of ὅτι.) What, therefore, must a person appropriate if he or she is to love others sincerely? What might you assume about a person who has difficulty loving others? (Cf. Luke 7:47.)

_____

_____

3. Schnackenburg notes that the argument in v. 20 is an *a fortiori* argument, a logical device that was common in the ancient rabbinic schools (*Epistles*, 226). Find the meaning of *a fortiori* in an English dictionary and explain how this logic is applied by John in the verse.

_____

_____

4. In v. 20, John states it is a contradiction to "hate" (μισέω) one's brother (ἀδελφός) while claiming to love God. Yet, according to Jesus (Luke 14:26), unless a person hates (μισέω) his family (including his "brothers," ἀδελφοί), he cannot be Jesus' disciple. Is there a legitimate place for hate in the Christian life? How would you resolve the apparent conflict concerning hate in the above two verses?

5. According to v. 21, to love is an ἐντολή, a "command" or "order" from God. Yet, many Christians seem to teach that for believers, love is supposed to be from the heart—free, spontaneous, unmotivated; one should love not because one *has* to but because one *wants* to. How would you resolve this enigma?

Faith Is the Victory
1 John 5:1–5

VOCABULARY

πιστεύων, pres. ptcp. act. masc. nom. sg. of πιστεύω, *the one who believes*

γεννήσαντα, aor. ptcp. act. masc. acc. sg. of γεννάω, *the one who gave birth, begat*

γεγεννημένον [v. 1], perf. ptcp. pass. masc. acc. sg. of γεννάω, *the one who has been born, begotten*

ὅταν, conj. used with the subj., *when, whenever*

ποιῶμεν, pres. subj. act. 1st pl. of ποιέω, *[when] we do, observe*

βαρεῖαι, fem. nom. pl. of the 1st and 3d decl. adj. βαρύς, -εῖα, -ύ, *heavy, burdensome, difficult.* Our English terms "baritone" and "barometer" are derived from this word's root.

γεγεννημένον [v. 4], perf. ptcp. pass. neut. nom. sg. of γεννάω, *[whatever] has been born, begotten*

νικᾷ, pres. indic. act. 3d sg. of νικάω, *he conquers, overcomes*

νίκη, -ης, ἡ, *victory*

νικήσασα, aor. ptcp. act. fem. nom. sg. of νικάω, *[that] conquered, overcame*

πίστις, 3d decl. fem. nom. sg. of πίστις, πίστεως, *faith, trust, belief*

νικῶν, pres. ptcp. act. masc. nom. sg. of νικάω, *the one who conquers, overcomes*

QUESTIONS

1. To what person does γεννήσαντα refer (v. 1)? Also γεγεννημένον (v. 1)? Pay particular attention to the voice of each participle.

_____

_____

2. Explain the mood of the two uses of ἀγαπῶμεν in v. 2.

3. Should θεοῦ in the phrase ἡ ἀγάπη τοῦ θεοῦ (v. 3) be construed as an objective or a subjective genitive? (See Dana and Mantey, *Manual Grammar*, §90.5.)

4. What idea is conveyed by the term βαρύς (v. 3)? (See *TDNT* 1:556–58.) What is John stressing by using this adjective in connection with God's commandments and our relation to them?

5. Why does John use the neuter form πᾶν in v. 4 of the one who is born of God? (See Marshall, *Epistles*, 228 n. 37.)

6. What does John mean in v. 4 by ἡ πίστις? Is he referring to the act of believing, to the facts believed by the Christian, or both? (See Haas, DeJonge, and Swellengrebel, *Translator's Handbook*, 117; Smalley, *1, 2, 3 John*, 271.)

7. Where else in John's writings does the verb νικάω (vv. 4–5) occur in regard to believers' being victorious? (Consult Kohlenberger, Goodrick, and Swanson's *Exhaustive Concordance.*)

_____

_____

_____

FOR FURTHER STUDY

1. Based on the tenses of the verbs πιστεύων and γεγέννηται in v. 1, is faith the cause of the new birth or its effect?

_____

_____

2. In v. 1, evidence that one is a true child of God comes through believing that Jesus is the Messiah (Χριστός). According to the Old Testament, is the Messiah depicted as a human figure or a divine figure? What role was the Messiah, Son of David, expected to perform? How closely did Jesus fulfill that expectation? In John's day some believed that Ἰησοῦς ἐστιν ὁ χριστός and others refused to believe. Does the New Testament, especially 1 John, shed any light on what made the difference between the two groups? Discuss.

_____

_____

3. Some Christians argue that the commandments or laws given by God to his people were a heavy burden, not a delight. In v. 3, however, John states that God's ἐντολαί, "commandments," are not βαρεῖαι, "burdensome." How does the theme of Psalm 119 compare with John's position? Furthermore, what perspective does the inauguration of the new age through Christ add to this question?

_____

_____

The Three Witnesses to the Son
1 John 5:6–12

VOCABULARY

ἐλθών, 2d aor. ptcp. act. masc. nom. sg. of ἔρχομαι, *[the one who] came*

ὕδατος, 3d decl. neut. gen. sg. of ὕδωρ, dat. ὕδατι, *water*

μαρτυροῦν, pres. ptcp. act. neut. nom. sg. of μαρτυρέω, *[who] is bearing witness*

μαρτυροῦντες, pres. ptcp. act. masc. nom. pl. of μαρτυρέω, *[who] are bearing witness*

τρεῖς, masc. nom. pl. of the 1st and 3d decl. adj. τρεῖς, τρία, *three*

εἰς τὸ ἕν εἰσιν, an idiom, literally: *are to the one thing*, and so *agree*

μεμαρτύρηκεν, perf. indic. act. 3d sg. of μαρτυρέω, *he has borne witness*

πεποίηκεν, perf. indic. act. 3d sg. of ποιέω, *he has made*

πεπίστευκεν, perf. indic. act. 3d sg. of πιστεύω, *he has [not] come to believe*

ἔχων, pres. ptcp. act. masc. nom. sg., *the one who has*

QUESTIONS

1. To what do ὕδωρ and αἷμα in v. 6 refer? (See Vincent, *Writings of John*, 364–65.) What teaching might this reference to water and blood have been meant to refute? (See Stott, *Letters*, 180–82; Johnson, *1, 2, 3 John*, 126.)

2. How should the prepositions διά and ἐν be interpreted in v. 6? (See Young, *Intermediate NT Greek*, 92–93.)

3. Why does John use the masculine participle μαρτυροῦντες (v. 7) when it refers to τὸ πνεῦμα καὶ τὸ ὕδωρ καὶ τὸ αἷμα, all neuter nouns? (See Marshall, *Epistles*, 237 n. 20; Wallace, *Grammar*, 332 n. 44.)

4. According to Zerwick (*Biblical Greek*, §32), what influenced the idiom in v. 8, τρεῖς εἰς τὸ ἕν εἰσιν (i.e., the use of εἰς + accusative in the place of the predicate nominative)? (See also Wallace, *Grammar*, 47.)

5. What is the implication of the condition in v. 9? (See Robertson, *Epistles*, 241.)

6. On the basis of the tense of the two participles in v. 10, what kind of belief does God expect from the Christian? (See Wallace, *Grammar*, 621 n. 22.)

7. What kind of clause is ὅτι ζωὴν αἰώνιον ἔδωκεν ἡμῖν ὁ θεός (v. 11; cf. v. 9)? (See Dana and Mantey, *Manual Grammar*, §281.1.) Explain its relation to the first clause in the sentence, καὶ αὕτη ἐστὶν ἡ μαρτυρία.

8. What is the sense conveyed by ἔχω in v. 12? (See Haas, DeJonge, and Swellengrebel, *Translator's Handbook*, 123.)

FOR FURTHER STUDY

1. What is the Old Testament background of John's reference to the testimony of three witnesses in v. 7? (See Deut 17:6; 19:15; cf. John 8:17–18.)

2. Verses 7–8 (known as the *Comma Johanneum*, i.e., "the Johannine [interpolated] clause") have been of special interest to the textual critic. After μαρτυροῦντες in v. 7 the Textus Receptus adds ἐν τῷ οὐρανῷ, ὁ πατήρ, ὁ λόγος, καὶ τὸ ἅγιον πνεῦμα, καὶ οὗτοι οἱ τρεῖς ἕν εἰσιν. (8) καὶ τρεῖς εἰσιν οἱ μαρτυροῦντες ἐν τῇ γῇ. The Textus Receptus is the Greek text upon which the King James Version (1611) was based. Read vv. 7–8 in the KJV and NKJV along with the discussion below of the external and internal evidence regarding the passage. Be sure to review the procedure textual critics use in their attempt to determine the original reading of the text (See Greenlee, *Textual Criticism*, 111–16; see also Metzger, *Text of the NT*, 209–11; Aland and Aland, *Text of the NT*, 280–82.) After studying the evidence, do you think this text as translated in the KJV/NKJV should be used as a proof text for the doctrine of the Trinity?

In deciding between textual variants two broad types of evidence must be considered: external and internal evidence.

External evidence includes the Greek manuscripts (hereafter: mss.), the various versions (translations of the New Testament into other languages, i.e., Latin, Coptic, Syriac, etc.), and the writings of the Fathers. It must be emphasized that the *quality*, not the *quantity*, of mss. is important for textual decisions. The most important mss. to be evaluated are the more than 5,000 extant Greek mss. These are evaluated according to date, geographical distribution, genealogical relationship (i.e., which ms. was copied from or is related to which other mss.), and scribal accuracy. These *qualities* are extremely important when making textual choices, for the reading of the largest number of mss. (the majority) is often a multiplication of an error. (For a discussion of the procedure for examining external evidence see Metzger, *Text of the NT*, 209; Greenlee, *Textual Criticism*, 114–16.)

Internal evidence supports arguments as to what the author is most likely to have written and what changes scribes are most likely to have made. Thus it includes discussion of the style and logical coherency of the text and also of "transcriptional probabilities." Several rules of thumb summarize the practice of modern text critics with regard to internal evidence:

The reading from which the other reading(s) most likely arose is probably original.

The shorter reading is usually preferred (with certain exceptions—see Greenlee, *Textual Criticism*, 112). Scribes were more likely to add to text that they thought was incomplete than to delete text that was already there.

A reading characterized by words or forms foreign to the author's style or flow of logic is suspect.

It must be remembered that these rules are only guidelines and that there may be exceptions. Each textual variant must be considered individually in the light of *all* available evidence. (For a discussion of the procedure for examining internal evidence see Metzger, *Text of the NT*, 209–11; Greenlee, *Textual Criticism*, 111–14.)

External Evidence for 1 John 5:7–8

a. Observe the textual notes for 1 John 5:7–8 at the bottom of the page of your Greek New Testament. It is clear that all but a few Greek mss. support the shorter reading of μαρτυροῦντες τὸ πνεῦμα καὶ τὸ ὕδωρ καὶ τὸ αἷμα. However, as has been stated above, we cannot found our case on the basis of a quantity (or majority) of mss. We must examine their quality as well.

b. The Greek mss. in support of the shorter reading *are* of good quality. They represent the earliest mss. (ℵ, B—4th cent.; A, 048—5th cent., etc.) as well as the widest geographical distribution. In contrast, the mss. supporting the longer reading are eight later mss.: 61—16th cent., 88mg—12th cent. (with the reading added to the margin [mg] by a 16th cent. hand), 221mg—10th cent. (with a marginal reading added by a later hand), 429mg—14th cent. (with the reading added to the margin by a later hand), 629—14th cent., 636mg—15th cent. (with a reading added to the margin by a later hand), 918—16th cent., 2318—18th cent. (dates taken from NA^{27}, 704–11). While all of these contain the longer reading, this evidence is very weak. None of these mss. date from before the 10th century and, as pointed out, four of them have the reading written in the margin by a later hand. It is probable that the reading arose when the original passage was interpreted as a symbol of the Trinity, an interpretation that was perhaps first written as a marginal note and later moved from the margin to the body of the text. (For the story of how the words came to be included in the Textus Receptus, see Metzger, *Text of the NT,* 101–102.)

c. The longer reading is quoted by none of the Greek Fathers. Had they known it they would have certainly employed it in the great Trinitarian controversies.

d. The passage in question is absent from all of the early versions (Syriac—2d–6th cent., Coptic—3d–4th cent., Armenian—4th–5th cent., Ethiopic—6th–8th cent., Georgian—5th–10th cent.) except the Latin. However, it is not found in the Old Latin in its early form (Tertullian, Cyprian, Augustine) or in Jerome's Vulgate (copied A.D. 541–546) or in Alcuin's revision (9th cent.).

e. The earliest reference to this passage is a quotation in a fourth-century Latin treatise attributed to Priscillian.

Internal Evidence for 1 John 5:7–8

a. If the passage in question were original, no good reason can be found to account for its omission from *all* the early Greek mss. and ancient versions except the Latin. It surely would not have been omitted, especially in light of the fact that the passage would have provided a good proof text for the Trinity.

b. The shorter passage complies with the rule for textual criticism that the shorter reading is to be preferred in light of the tendency of scribes to add rather than delete.

c. The disputed words disrupt the logic of the passage. Verse 8 speaks of a threefold witness that satisfies the requirement of the law (see Deut 17:6; 19:15) applicable among men. Verse 9 proceeds to refer to the witness of God, which is greater. Inserting the questionable portion here breaks this logical progression of thought.

3. What light is shed by the tense of the four verbal forms in v. 12 on the question of whether or not eternal life is the present possession of every believer in Christ? (Note also the tense of ἔχετε in v. 13.)

_____

_____

_____

_____

Promise of Eternal Life
1 John 5:13–17

Vocabulary

εἰδῆτε, 2d perf. subj. act. 2d pl. of οἶδα, *[that] you might know*

πιστεύουσιν, pres. ptcp. act. masc. dat. pl. of πιστεύω, *[to those who] believe*

αἰτώμεθα, pres. subj. mid. 1st pl. of αἰτέω, *[if] we ask, request*

αἴτημα, αἰτήματος, τό, *request, what is asked for.* See Phil 4:6.

ἠτήκαμεν, perf. indic. act. 1st pl. of αἰτέω, *we have asked, requested*

ἴδῃ, 2d aor. subj. act. 3d sg. of ὁράω, *[if anyone] sees*

ἁμαρτάνοντα, pres. ptcp. act. masc. acc. sg. of ἁμαρτάνω, *[the one] sinning*

δώσει, fut. indic. act. 3d sg. of δίδωμι, *he will give*

ἁμαρτάνουσιν, pres. ptcp. act. masc. dat. pl. of ἁμαρτάνω, *[to those who] are sinning*

ἐρωτήσῃ, aor. subj. act. 3d sg. of ἐρωτάω, *[that] he should ask, make request*

Questions

1. What is being emphasized in v. 13 when the verb ἔχετε separates ζωήν and αἰώνιον? (See Smalley, *1, 2, 3 John,* 290.)

2. According to Smalley (*1, 2, 3 John*, 295), what is the significance of the continual use of the first person plural throughout vv. 14–15 (and in vv. 18–20)?

3. What is the significance of the verb οἶδα occurring twice in v. 15? (See Schnackenburg, *Epistles*, 247.)

4. How do you explain the use of ἐάν with the indicative οἴδαμεν in the protasis of the condition in v. 15? (See Burton, *Syntax*, §247; Zerwick, *Biblical Greek*, §331.)

5. What kind of accusative is αἰτήματα in v. 15? ἁμαρτίαν in v. 16? (See Brooks and Winbery, *Syntax*, 50–51; Wallace, *Grammar*, 189–90.)

6. How should πρὸς θάνατον in v. 16 be translated (cf. John 11:4)? (See *NIDNTT* 3:1206.)

7. Why are two different negatives (μή and οὐκ) used in vv. 16 and 17 to express "not to death"? What basic rules of Greek grammar apply here? (See Wenham, *Elements*, 248.15.) Is there a difference in meaning between ἁμαρτίαν μὴ πρὸς θάνατον (v. 16) and ἁμαρτία οὐ πρὸς θάνατον (v. 17)? (See Turner, *Syntax*, 281.)

_____

_____

8. How should καί be understood in v. 17? (See Zerwick and Grosvenor, *Grammatical Analysis*, 733; BDF §442.1.)

_____

_____

_____

For Further Study

1. Verse 14 states that for God to hear a believer's requests the believer must pray κατὰ τὸ θέλημα αὐτοῦ. Discuss what this expression means as a precondition for answered prayer.

_____

_____

2. There is a sin that leads to death (v. 16). What do you think that sin is? Why? In formulating your answer be sure to make use of the principle of exegesis which calls for a careful study of the passage in relation to the chapter, book, group of writings, and Testament where it is found. The analogy of Scripture (comparing Scripture with Scripture) should provide considerable help in understanding the various alternatives for interpreting this passage. (For help, see *NIDNTT* 3:1205–6; Stott, *Letters*, 189–93.)

_____

_____

_____

3. One of the main purposes John has in writing to believers is to assure them, ἵνα εἰδῆτε ὅτι ζωὴν ἔχετε αἰώνιον (v. 13). Today, if a believer states to an unbeliever, "I *know* I have eternal life," it may come across as arrogant and presumptuous. Indeed, in this day and age, characterized by relativism and agnosticism, to "know" something sounds too absolute for many people. Putting yourself in the context of John's day, discuss why he had such great concern about imparting knowledge of eternal life. If John were writing to our generation, do you think he might temper his statement or word things somewhat differently? Discuss.

The Things One Born of God Really Knows
1 John 5:18–21

VOCABULARY

γεννηθείς, aor. ptcp. pass. masc. nom. sg. of γεννάω, [the one who] was born, begotten

ἄπτω, light, set on fire; middle: touch, fasten oneself to, cling to, take hold of

κεῖμαι, lie, be, exist

ἥκω, be present

διάνοια, -ας, ἡ, understanding, mind, intelligence

φυλάξατε, aor. impv. act. 2d pl. of φυλάσσω, guard, keep

εἴδωλον, -ου, τό, idol. It is derived from ἰδεῖν, to see.

QUESTIONS

1. Discuss the tense of the participles in v. 18.

2. What is the case and use of αὐτοῦ in v. 18? (See BDF §170.)

3. What sense does the verb κεῖται convey in v. 19? (See Smalley, *1, 2, 3 John*, 305.)

_____

_____

4. With what phrase in v. 20 does the phrase ἐν τῷ πονηρῷ (v. 19) stand in contrast?

_____

_____

5. Where else in the New Testament do the words φυλάσσω ἀπό occur together as they do in v. 21? (See Kohlenberger, Goodrick, and Swanson, *Exhaustive Concordance.*)

_____

_____

6. Why is ἑαυτά (v. 21) neuter? What is its antecedent? What does its use here emphasize? (See Smalley, *1, 2, 3 John*, 309.)

_____

_____

7. In v. 21, εἰδώλων may be translated "false gods" rather than "images" or "idols." From the context (especially the preceding verse), can you make a case for the translation "false gods"?

_____

_____

8. The KJV concludes this letter with the word "Amen" (v. 21). What textual support is there in the Greek for this word? (See Metzger, *Textual Commentary*, 651.)

_____

_____

_____

For Further Study

1. Who is the antecedent of the demonstrative οὗτος in v. 20, God the Father or Christ? The answer to this question is relevant to the issue of whether or not Christ is being referred to by John here as ὁ ἀληθινὸς θεός. Consider the following as you seek to formulate your answer:

   a. What is the closest referent to οὗτος?

   _____

   _____

   b. Consult Kohlenberger, Goodrick, and Swanson (*Exhaustive Concordance*) to see how often the demonstrative οὗτος is used of Christ in this epistle and in John's other writings and whether it is ever used of the Father by John.

   _____

   _____

   c. Has Christ been referred to as the "eternal life" elsewhere in the epistle? (Note: this epithet is never used of the Father in the New Testament.)

   _____

   _____

   d. In light of the answer to the previous question, how might Granville Sharp's rule be relevant to the interpretation of v. 20? (According to the rule, the two predicate complements, ὁ ἀληθινὸς θεός and ζωὴ αἰώνιος would be referring to the same person; see Wallace, *Grammar*, 70.)

   _____

   _____

   _____

e. Would Christ's being God explain how one can be in the Father
(ὁ ἀληθινός) by being in the Son (v. 20)?

_____

_____

_____

_____

f. Would an affirmation of Christ's deity at the beginning (1:1–2) and
here at the end of his epistle be fitting in light of the manner in
which John begins and concludes his gospel (cf. John 1:1; 20:28)?

_____

_____

_____

2. Note the relation of the verb φυλάσσω (v. 21) to the term φυλακτήρια
("phylacteries") in Matt 23:5. What are phylacteries (or *tephillin*)? Ob-
servant Jews at the time of Christ would have worn phylacteries. This
was in accord with Moses' command to all Israel (Deut 6:8). Do some
reading on the meaning of this passage in an Old Testament commentary or Bible dictionary or encyclopedia. How does the meaning of the
root φυλάσσω relate to the noun φυλακτήρια and the ritual Jewish
practice of using phylacteries?

_____

_____

_____

3. Three of the final four verses of 1 John (vv. 18–21) begin with οἴδαμεν
as John again summarizes what one born of God really knows. What
does John say true believers hold with certainty?

_____

_____

_____

GREEK-ENGLISH DICTIONARY OF FIRST JOHN

Numbers in parentheses refer to the assignments where the word is introduced or discussed.

A

ἀγαπάω, ἀγαπήσω, ἠγάπησα, ἠγάπηκα, ἠγάπημαι, ἠγαπήθην, *love* (5, 7, 13, 14, 19, 20, 21, 22)

ἀγάπη, -ης, ἡ, *love* (19, 21, 22)

ἀγαπητός, -ή, -όν, *beloved, dear(est)* (5, 19)

ἀγγελία, -ας, ἡ, *message, news* (2, 13)

ἅγιος, -α, -ον, *holy*

ἁγνίζω, ———, ἥγνισα, ἥγνικα, ἥγνισμαι, ἡγνίσθην, *purify, cleanse* (11)

ἁγνός, -ή, -όν, *pure, clean, holy* (11)

ἀδελφός, -οῦ, ὁ, *brother, fellow believer* (5, 14, 15, 21)

ἀδικία, -ας, ἡ, *unrighteousness, injustice, wrong, evil, iniquity* (3)

αἷμα, -ατος, τό, *blood* (2, 23)

αἴρω, ἀρῶ, ἦρα, ἦρκα, ἦρμαι, ἤρθην, *take up, take away, remove* (12)

αἰσχύνω, ———, ———, ———, ———, ᾐσχύνθην, *be ashamed, be put to shame, be made ashamed* (10)

αἰτέω, αἰτήσω, ᾔτησα, ᾔτηκα, *ask, request* (16, 24)

αἴτημα, -ατος, τό, *request, what is asked for* (24)

αἰών, αἰῶνος, ὁ, *eternity, age;* εἰς τὸν αἰῶνα, *forever* (7)

αἰώνιος, -ον, *eternal, everlasting* (1, 7, 9, 23, 24)

ἀκούω, ἀκούσω, ἤκουσα, ἀκήκοα, ———, ἠκούσθην, *hear, listen* (takes gen. or acc. object) (1, 17, 18)

ἀλαζονεία, -ας, ἡ, *boastfulness, vain display, pretension, arrogance, pride* (7)

ἀλήθεια, -ας, ἡ, *truth, truthfulness* (15, 18)

ἀληθής, -ές, *true, truthful, real, genuine* (5)

ἀληθινός, -ή, -όν, *real, genuine, true, dependable* (5, 25)

ἀληθῶς, *truly, surely, certainly* (4)

ἀλλά, *but, rather* (17)

ἀλλήλων, -οις, -ους, *one another, each other* (19)

ἁμαρτάνω, ἁμαρτήσω, ἡμάρτησα or ἥμαρτον, ἡμάρτηκα, *sin* (3, 4, 12, 13, 24)

ἁμαρτία, -ας, ἡ, *sin* (3, 4, 12, 24)

ἄν, a particle denoting contingency in certain clause constructions; not translated separately into English (4, 8) ἀναγγέλλω, ἀναγγελῶ, ἀνήγγειλα, ———, ———, ἀνηγγέλην, *proclaim, declare, announce, report* (2)

ἀνθρωποκτόνος, -ου, ὁ, *murderer* (14)

ἄνθρωπος, -ου, ὁ, *man, human being, person*

ἀνομία, -ας, ἡ, *lawlessness, transgression, wickedness* (12)

ἀντίχριστος, -ου, ὁ, *antichrist* (8, 17)

ἀπαγγέλλω, ἀπαγγελῶ, ἀπήγγειλα, ———, ———, ἀπηγγέλην, *announce, report, inform, proclaim* (1)

ἀπό, prep. with gen., *from, away from* (6, 10, 12, 25)

ἀποστέλλω, ἀποστελῶ, ἀπέστειλα, ἀπέσταλκα, ἀπέσταλμαι, ἀπεστάλην, *send, send forth, send away* (19)

ἅπτω, ———, ἧψα, *light, set on fire;* mid., *touch, fasten oneself to, cling to, take hold of* (25)

ἀρεστός, -ή, -όν, *pleasing, agreeable, acceptable* (16)

ἀρνέομαι, ἀρνήσομαι, ἠρνησάμην, ———, ἤρνημαι, *deny, disown, renounce* (9)

ἄρτι, *now, at the present time* (5)

ἀρχή, -ῆς, ἡ, *beginning, first* (1, 6, 12)

αὐτός, -ή, -ό, *he, she, it, himself, herself, itself, same* (3, 4, 5, 7, 8, 9, 15, 16, 20, 24, 25)

ἀφίημι, ἀφήσω, ἀφῆκα, ἀφεῖκα, ἀφεῖμαι, ἀφέθην, *forgive, remit, cancel, allow, let go, send away* (3, 6)

B

βάλλω, βαλῶ, ἔβαλον, βέβληκα, βέβλημαι, ἐβλήθην, *throw, put, place, cast, banish*

βαρύς, -εῖα, -ύ, *heavy, burdensome, difficult* (22)

βίος, -ου, ὁ, *life, period of life, means of living, property, possessions* (7)

Γ

γάρ, *for, since, indeed*

γεννάω, γεννήσω, ἐγέννησα, γεγέννηκα, γεγέννημαι, ἐγεννήθην, *give birth to, beget, bear;* pass., *be born* (10, 13, 22, 25)

γίνομαι, γενήσομαι, ἐγενόμην, γέγονα, γεγένημαι, ἐγενήθην, *become, am, happen, arise, come into being, appear* (8)

γινώσκω, γνώσομαι, ἔγνων, ἔγνωκα, ἔγνωσμαι, ἐγνώσθην, *know, come to know, understand, perceive* (4, 11, 12, 18, 19, 20)

γλῶσσα, -ης, ἡ, *tongue, speech, language* (15)

γράφω, γράψω, ἔγραψα, γέγραφα, γέγραμμαι, ἐγράφην, *write* (6)

Δ

δέ, *but, and, now* (17)

διά, prep. with gen., *by, through;* with acc., *because of, on account of* (23)

διάβολος, -ου, ὁ, *devil, slanderer* (12, 13)

διάνοια, -ας ἡ, *understanding, mind, intelligence* (25)
διδάσκω, διδάξω, ἐδίδαξα, ———, ———, ἐδιδάχθην, *teach* (10)
δίδωμι, δώσω, ἔδωκα, δέδωκα, δέδομαι, ἐδόθην, *give* (11, 16, 23, 24)
δίκαιος, -α, -ον, *righteous, just* (3)
δικαιοσύνη, -ης, ἡ, *righteousness, what is right*
δοκιμάζω, δοκιμάσω, ἐδοκίμασα, ———, δεδοκίμασμαι, *test, examine, prove, ap-*
    prove (17)
δύναμαι, δυνήσομαι, ———, ———, ———, ἠδυνήθην, *be able, capable of, can* (13)

E

ἐάν, *if* (2, 15, 24)
ἑαυτοῦ, -ῆς, -οῦ, *himself, herself, itself* (3, 25)
ἐγώ, ἐμοῦ, (μου) ἐμοί (μοι) ἐμέ (με), *I, me*
εἰ, *if, whether;* εἰ μή, *if not, except* (9, 14, 17)
εἴδωλον, -ου, τό, *idol, image, false god* (25)
εἰμί, ἔσομαι; impf. ἤμην (1st sg.) and ἦν (3rd sg.), *be* (5, 11, 19, 23)
εἰς, prep. with acc., *into, in, to, towards, for* (16, 23)
εἷς, μία, ἕν, *one;* εἰς τὸ ἕν εἰσιν, *agree* (23)
ἐκ (ἐξ), prep. with gen., *from, out from, of* (7, 8, 16, 18, 20, 22)
ἐκεῖνος, -η, -ο, *that [one]; he, she, it* (4, 12)
ἐλπίς, ἐλπίδος, ἡ, *hope* (11)
ἔμπροσθεν, prep. with gen., *in front of, before* (15)
ἐν, prep. with dat., *in, by* (18, 19, 23, 25)
ἐντολή, -ῆς, ἡ, *commandment, command, order* (5, 16, 21)
ἐνώπιον, prep. with gen., *before, in the presence of* (16)
ἐξέρχομαι, ἐξελεύσομαι, ἐξῆλθον, ἐξελήλυθα, *come out, go out*
ἔξω, *out, without, outside, away* (21)
ἐπαγγελία, -ας, ἡ, *promise* (9)
ἐπαγγέλλομαι, ———, ἐπηγγειλάμην, ———, ἐπήγγελμαι, *promise* (9)
ἐπί, prep. with gen., *on, upon, over;* with dat., *on, at, in, with, by, near;* with acc., *on,*
    to, against (11)
ἐπιθυμία, -ας, ἡ, *strong desire, longing, lust* (7)
ἔργον, -ου, τό, *work, deed, action* (15)
ἔρχομαι, ἐλεύσομαι, ἦλθον, ἐλήλυθα, *come, go* (5, 17, 23)
ἐρωτάω, ἐρωτήσω, ἠρώτησα, *ask, request* (24)
ἔσχατος, -η, -ον, *last, final* (8)
ἔχω, ἔξω, ἔσχον, ἔσχηκα, impf. εἶχον, *have, hold, possess* (1, 3, 5, 10, 15, 21, 23, 24)
ἕως, conj., *until, while;* prep. with gen., *until, as far as* (5)

Z

ζάω, ζήσω, ἔζησα, *live, be alive* (19)
ζωή, -ῆς, ἡ, *life* (1, 7, 9, 14, 23, 24)

H

ἤ, *than, or* (18)
ἤδη, *now, already* (5, 17)
ἥκω, ἥξω, ἥξα, *have come, be present* (25)
ἡμεῖς, ἡμῶν, *we* (1, 15, 18, 19, 23)
ἡμέρα, -ας, ἡ, *day*
ἡμέτερος, -α, -ον, *our* (1)

Θ

θάνατος, -ου, ὁ, *death* (14, 24)
θαυμάζω, θαυμάσομαι, ἐθαύμασα, ———, ———, ἐθαυμάσθην, *wonder, marvel*
    (14)
θεάομαι, ———, ἐθεασάμην, ———, τεθέαμαι, ἐθεάθην, *behold, look at, see* (1, 20)
θέλημα, -ατος, τό, *will, wish, desire* (7, 24)
θεός, -οῦ, ὁ, *God, god* (18, 19, 20, 22, 23, 25)
θεωρέω, θεωρήσω, ἐθεώρησα, *see, observe, look at* (15)

I

Ἰησοῦς, -οῦ, ὁ, *Jesus* (20)
ἱλασμός, -οῦ, ὁ, *propitiation, means of appeasing wrath, sin-offering, atoning sacrifice*
    (4, 19)
ἵνα, *that, in order that, to* (3, 11, 16)
ἰσχυρός, -ά, -όν, *powerful, mighty, strong* (6)

K

καθαρίζω, καθαριῶ, ἐκαθάρισα, ———, κεκαθάρισμαι, ἐκαθαρίσθην, *cleanse,*
    make clean, purify (2, 3)
καθώς, *as, just as* (4)
καί, *and, even, also, but, namely;* καὶ . . . καί, *both . . . and, not only . . . but also* (5, 11,
    21, 24)
Κάϊν, ὁ, *Cain* (13)
καινός, -ή, -όν, *new, fresh, unused* (5)
καλέω, καλέσω, ἐκάλεσα, κέκληκα, κέκλημαι, ἐκλήθην, *call* (11)
καρδία, -ας, ἡ, *heart* (15, 16)
κατά, prep. with gen., *down from, against;* with acc., *according to, through, by* (24)
καταγινώσκω, ———, ———, ———, κατέγνωσμαι, *condemn* (15, 16)
κεῖμαι, *lie, be, exist* (25)
κλείω, κλείσω, ἔκλεισα, ———, κέκλεισμαι, ἐκλείσθην, *shut, close* (15)

κοινωνία, -ας, ἡ, *fellowship, participation, sharing, communion* (1, 2)
κόλασις, -εως, ἡ, *punishment, correction, penalty* (21)
κόσμος, -ου, ὁ, *world, universe, mankind* (7, 18)
κρίσις, -εως, ἡ, *judgment, decision, right* (in the sense of justice) (21)

Λ

λαλέω, λαλήσω, ἐλάλησα, λελάληκα, λελάλημαι, ἐλαλήθην, *speak, say, tell*
λαμβάνω, λήμψομαι, ἔλαβον, εἴληφα, εἴλημμαι, ἐλήμφθην, *take, receive* (16)
λέγω, ἐρῶ, εἶπον, εἴρηκα, εἴρημαι, ἐρρέθην, *say, speak, tell* (2, 4, 21)
λόγος, -ου, ὁ, *word* (3, 6, 15)
λύω, λύσω, ἔλυσα, λέλυκα, λέλυμαι, ἐλύθην, *destroy, loose* (12)

Μ

μαρτυρέω, μαρτυρήσω, ἐμαρτύρησα, μεμαρτύρηκα, μεμαρτύρημαι, ἐμαρτυρήθην,
  bear witness, witness, testify, be a witness (1, 20, 23)
μαρτυρία, -ας, ἡ, *witness, testimony, evidence* (23)
μείζων, -ον, *greater* (comp. of μέγας) (15, 18)
μένω, μενῶ, ἔμεινα, μεμένηκα, *abide, dwell, live, remain* (4, 8, 9, 10, 12, 14, 20)
μετά, prep. with gen., *with;* with acc., *after*
μεταβαίνω, μεταβήσομαι, μετέβην, μεταβέβηκα, *pass over, cross over, move* (14)
μή, *not* (normally used with non-indicative verbs) (9, 14, 24)
μηδέ, *nor, and not, not even;* μηδὲ . . . μηδέ, *neither* . . . nor
μηδείς, μηδεμία, μηδέν, *no one, nothing*
μισέω, μισήσω, ἐμίσησα, μεμίσηκα, μεμίσημαι, *hate, despise* (5, 21)
μονογενής, -ές, *only, only begotten, unique* (19)
μόνον, *only, alone* (4)

Ν

νεανίσκος, -ου, ὁ, *young man, youth* (6)
νικάω, νικήσω, ἐνίκησα, νενίκηκα, ———, ἐνικήθην, *conquer, overcome, win the vic-*
  tory over (6, 18, 22)
νίκη, -ης, ἡ, *victory* (22)
νῦν, *now, at the present* (17)

Ο

ὁ, ἡ, τό; pl. οἱ, αἱ, τά, *the* (7)
ὅθεν, *whence, wherefore, from where* (8)

οἶδα (2d perf. used as pres.); εἰδήσω (fut.); ᾔδειν (2d pluperf.), *know* (5, 8, 10, 11, 24, 25)

ὅλος, -η, -ον, *whole, all, complete, entire* (4)

ὅμοιος, -α, -ον, *like, similar to, of the same nature as* (11)

ὁμολογέω, ὁμολογήσω, ὡμολόγησα, *confess, acknowledge, admit, declare publicly* (3, 9, 20)

ὄνομα, -ατος, τό, *name* (6, 16)

ὁράω, ὄψομαι, εἶδον, ἑώρακα or ἑόρακα, ———, ὤφθην, *see* (1, 11, 12, 24)

ὅς, ἥ, ὅ, *who, which, what, that* (1, 4, 5, 16)

ὅστις, ἥτις, ὅ τι, *who, which; whoever, whichever, whatever* (1)

ὅταν, *when, whenever* (22)

ὅτι, *that, because;* may mark the beginning of direct discourse (2, 5, 6, 15, 19, 21)

οὐ, οὐκ, οὐχ, *not* (2, 9, 24)

οὐδέ, *neither, nor, and not, not even* (9)

οὐδείς, οὐδεμία, οὐδέν, *no one, nobody, nothing, no* (2, 9)

οὔπω, *not yet* (11)

οὗτος, αὕτη, τοῦτο, *this, this one, he, she, it* (1, 11, 13, 18, 23, 25)

οὕτως, *thus, so, in this way, like this* (4, 20)

ὀφείλω, *owe, be obligated, ought* (4, 15)

ὀφθαλμός, -οῦ, ὁ, *eye* (1, 7)

Π

παιδίον, -ου, τό, *child, little child, young child* (6)

παλαιός, -ά, -όν, *old, ancient, former* (5)

πάλιν, *again, once more, yet, on the other hand* (5)

παράγω, *pass by* (in act.); *pass away, disappear, be brought past* (in pass.) (5)

παράκλητος, -ου, ὁ, *advocate, intercessor, helper, one who speaks in another's defense* (4)

παρουσία, -ας, ἡ, *presence, coming, arrival* (10)

παρρησία, -ας, ἡ, *boldness, openness, confidence* (10)

πᾶς, πᾶσα, πᾶν, *all, every* (2, 8, 9, 10, 22)

πατήρ, πατρός, ὁ, *father* (1, 6, 9)

πείθω, πείσω, ἔπεισα, πέποιθα, πέπεισμαι, ἐπείσθην, *persuade, convince, reassure* (15)

περί, prep. with gen., *concerning, about, for, with reference to* (4)

περιπατέω, περιπατήσω, περιεπάτησα, περιπεπάτηκα, *walk, live, conduct oneself* (2, 4)

πιστεύω, πιστεύσω, ἐπίστευσα, πεπίστευκα, πεπίστευμαι, ἐπιστεύθην, *believe, trust, have faith in* (16, 17, 21, 22, 23, 24)

πίστις, -εως, ἡ, *faith, trust, belief* (22)

πιστός, -ή, -όν, *faithful, reliable, trustworthy* (3)

πλανάω, πλανήσω, ἐπλάνησα, ———, πεπλάνημαι, ἐπλανήθην, *lead astray, deceive* (3, 10, 12, 18)

πλάνη, -ης, ἡ, *error, deceit, going astray, wandering* (18) πληρόω, πληρώσω, ἐπλήρωσα, πεπλήρωκα, πεπλήρωμαι, ἐπληρώθην, *fulfill, make full, fill, complete* (1)

πνεῦμα, -ατος, τό, *Spirit, spirit, wind* (16, 17, 18, 20, 23)

ποιέω, ποιήσω, ἐποίησα, πεποίηκα, πεποίημαι, ἐποιήθην, *do,* make (5, 7, 10, 12, 13, 16, 22, 23)

πολύς, πολλή, πολύ; *much;* pl. *many*

πονηρός, -ά, -όν, *evil, wicked, bad* (6, 25)

ποταπός, -ή, -όν, *what? of what sort? what kind of?* (11)

ποῦ, *where?* (5)

πρός, prep. with acc., *to, towards, with* (1, 24)

πρῶτος, -η, -ον, *first*

πώποτε, *ever, ever yet, at any time* (20)

πῶς, *how?* (15)

Σ

σάρξ, σαρκός, ἡ, *flesh* (7)

σκάνδαλον, -ου, τό, *stumbling block, cause of sin, that which causes stumbling* (5)

σκοτία, -ας, ἡ, *darkness* (2)

σκότος, -ους, τό, *darkness* (2)

σπέρμα, -ατος, τό, *seed, offspring, posterity, descendants* (13)

σπλάγχνον, -ου, τό, pl. τὰ σπλάγχνα, *inward parts, entrails, heart, affections, seat of emotions* (15)

σφάζω, σφάξω, ἔσφαξα, ———, ἔσφαγμαι, ἐσφάγην, *slaughter, slay, murder* (13)

σωτήρ, -ῆρος, ὁ, *savior, preserver, deliverer* (20)

Τ

τεκνίον, -ου, τό, *little child* (4, 6)

τέκνον, -ου, τό, *child* (13)

τέλειος, -α, -ον, *complete, mature, perfect* (21)

τελειόω, ———, ἐτελείωσα, τετελείωκα, τετελείωμαι, ἐτελειώθην, *complete, perfect, finish, accomplish* (4, 20, 21)

τηρέω, τηρήσω, ἐτήρησα, τετήρηκα, τετήρημαι, ἐτηρήθην, *keep, obey, observe, guard* (4, 16)

τίθημι, θήσω, ἔθηκα, τέθεικα, τέθειμαι, ἐτέθην, *place, put, lay down, give up* (15, 20)

τίς, τί, *who? which? what?* (9, 11)

τις, τι, *someone, anyone, a certain one* (masc. and fem.); *something, anything, a certain thing* (neut.) (4)

τρεῖς, τρία, *three* (23)

τυφλόω, ———, ἐτύφλωσα, τετύφλωκα, *blind, make blind* (5)

Υ

ὕδωρ, ὕδατος, τό, *water* (23)
υἱός, -οῦ, ὁ, *son* (19, 20)
ὑμεῖς, ὑμῶν, *you* (pl.) (8, 9, 18)
ὑπάγω, *go, go away, depart, leave* (5)
ὑπέρ, prep. with gen., *for, in behalf of, for the sake of;* with acc., *over, beyond* (15)

Φ

φαίνω, φανοῦμαι, ἔφανα, ———, ———, ἐφάνην, *shine, give light* (5)
φανερός, -ά, -όν, *visible, clear, plainly to be seen, known* (13)
φανερόω, φανερώσω, ἐφανέρωσα, πεφανέρωκα, πεφανέρωμαι, ἐφανερώθην, *reveal, make known, show, manifest, make manifest;* in pass., *be revealed, made known, become visible, appear* (1, 8, 10, 11)
φοβέομαι; aor. ἐφοβήθην, *fear, be afraid* (21)
φόβος, -ου, ὁ, *fear* (21)
φυλάσσω, φυλάξω, ἐφύλαξα, πεφύλακα, ———, ἐφυλάχθην, *guard,* keep, *protect* (25)
φῶς, φωτός, τό, *light* (2)

Χ

χαρά, -ᾶς, ἡ, *joy*
χάριν, prep. with gen., *for, on account of, for the sake of, because of* (13)
χείρ, χειρός, ἡ, *hand* (1)
χρεία, -ας, ἡ, *need, necessity* (10, 15)
χρῖσμα, -ατος, τό, *anointing, anointment* (8)
χριστός, -οῦ, ὁ, *Christ, Messiah, anointed* (8, 20, 22)

Ψ

ψεύδομαι, ψεύσομαι, ἐψευσάμην, *lie, deceive by lies, speak untruth* (2)
ψευδοπροφήτης, -ου, ὁ, *false prophet* (17)
ψεῦδος, -ους, τό, *lie, falsehood* (8)
ψεύστης, -ου, ὁ, *liar* (3)
ψηλαφάω, ———, ἐψηλάφησα, *feel, touch, handle* (1)
ψυχή, -ῆς, ἡ, *life, soul* (15)

Ω

ὥρα, -ας, ἡ, *hour, occasion, time* (8)
ὡς, *as* (2)

ANALYTICAL LEXICON OF FIRST JOHN

A

ἅ neut. acc. pl. ὅς, ἥ, ὅ

ἀγαπᾷ 3d sg. pres. ind./subj. act. ἀγαπάω

ἀγαπᾶν pres. inf. act. ἀγαπάω

ἀγαπᾶτε 2d pl. pres. impv./ind./subj. act. ἀγαπάω

ἀγάπη fem. nom. sg. ἀγάπη

ἀγάπῃ fem. dat. sg. ἀγάπη

ἀγάπην fem. acc. sg. ἀγάπη

ἀγαπητοί masc. voc./nom. pl. ἀγαπητός

ἀγαπῶ 1st sg. pres. ind./subj. act. ἀγαπάω

ἀγαπῶμεν 1st pl. pres. ind./subj. act. ἀγαπάω

ἀγαπῶν pres. ptcp. act. masc. nom. sg. ἀγαπάω

ἀγγελία fem. nom. sg. ἀγγελία

ἁγίου masc./neut. gen. sg. ἅγιος

ἁγνίζει 3d sg. pres. ind. act. ἁγνίζω

ἁγνός masc. nom. sg. ἁγνός

ἀδελφοί masc. voc. pl. ἀδελφός

ἀδελφόν masc. acc. sg. ἀδελφός

ἀδελφοῦ masc. gen. sg. ἀδελφός

ἀδελφούς masc. acc. pl. ἀδελφός

ἀδελφῶν masc. gen. pl. ἀδελφός

ἀδικία fem. nom. sg. ἀδικία

ἀδικίας fem. gen. sg. ἀδικία

αἱ fem. nom. pl. ὁ, ἡ, τό

αἷμα neut. nom./acc. sg. αἷμα

αἵματι neut. dat. sg. αἷμα

αἵματος neut. gen. sg. αἷμα

αἰσχυνθῶμεν 1st pl. aor. subj. pass. αἰσχύνω

αἰτήματα neut. nom./acc. pl. αἴτημα

αἰτήσει 3d sg. fut. ind. act. αἰτέω

αἰτώμεθα 1st pl. pres. subj. mid. αἰτέω

αἰτῶμεν 1st pl. pres. subj. act. αἰτέω

αἰῶνα masc. acc. sg. αἰών

αἰώνιον masc./fem./neut. acc. sg. αἰώνιος

ἀκηκόαμεν 1st pl. 2d perf. ind. act. ἀκούω

ἀκηκόατε 2d pl. 2d perf. ind. act. ἀκούω

ἀκούει 3d sg. pres. ind. act. ἀκούω

ἀλαζονεία fem. nom. sg. ἀλαζονεία

ἀλήθεια fem. nom. sg. ἀλήθεια

ἀληθείᾳ fem. dat. sg. ἀλήθεια

ἀλήθειαν fem. acc. sg. ἀλήθεια

ἀληθείας fem. gen. sg. ἀλήθεια

ἀληθές neut. nom./acc. sg. ἀληθής

ἀληθινόν neut./masc. nom./acc. sg. ἀληθινός

ἀληθινός masc. nom. sg. ἀληθινός

ἀληθινῷ masc./neut. dat. sg. ἀληθινός

ἀληθῶς adv. ἀληθῶς

ἀλλ᾽ conj. ἀλλά

ἀλλά conj. ἀλλά

ἀλλήλους masc. acc. pl. ἀλλήλων

ἀλλήλων masc./fem./neut. gen. pl. ἀλλήλων

ἁμαρτάνει 3d sg. pres. ind. act. ἁμαρτάνω

ἁμαρτάνειν pres. inf. act. ἁμαρτάνω

ἁμαρτάνοντα pres. ptcp. act. masc. acc. sg. ἁμαρτάνω

ἁμαρτάνουσιν pres. ptcp. act. masc./neut. dat. pl. ἁμαρτάνω

ἁμαρτάνων pres. ptcp. act. masc. nom. sg. ἁμαρτάνω

ἁμάρτῃ 3d sg. aor. subj. act. ἁμαρτάνω

ἁμάρτητε 2d pl. aor. subj. act. ἁμαρτάνω

ἁμαρτία fem. nom. sg. ἁμαρτία

ἁμαρτίαι fem. nom. pl. ἁμαρτία

ἁμαρτίαν fem. acc. sg. ἁμαρτία

ἁμαρτίας fem. gen./acc. sg. (gen.) or pl. (acc.) ἁμαρτία

ἁμαρτιῶν fem. gen. pl. ἁμαρτία

ἄν particle ἄν

ἀναγγέλλομεν 1st pl. pres. ind. act. ἀναγγέλλω

ἀνθρωποκτόνος masc. nom. sg. ἀνθρωποκτόνος

ἀνθρώπων masc. gen. pl. ἄνθρωπος

ἀνομία fem. nom. sg. ἀνομία

ἀνομίαν fem. acc. sg. ἀνομία

ἀντίχριστοι masc. nom. pl. ἀντίχριστος

ἀντίχριστος masc. nom. sg. ἀντίχριστος

ἀντιχρίστου masc. gen. sg. ἀντίχριστος

ἀπ᾽ prep. ἀπό

ἀπαγγέλλομεν 1st pl. pres. ind. act. ἀπαγγέλλω

ἀπέσταλκεν 3d sg. perf. ind. act. ἀποστέλλω

ἀπέστειλεν 3d sg. aor. ind. act. ἀποστέλλω

ἀπό prep. ἀπό

ἅπτεται 3d sg. pres. ind. mid. ἅπτω

ἀρεστά neut. nom./acc. pl. ἀρεστός

ἄρῃ 3d sg. aor. subj. act. αἴρω

ἀρνούμενος pres. mid. ptcp. masc. nom. sg. ἀρνέομαι

ἄρτι adv. ἄρτι

ἀρχῆς fem. gen. sg. ἀρχή

αὕτη fem. nom. sg. οὗτος, αὕτη, τοῦτο

αὐτήν fem. acc. sg. αὐτός, αὐτή, αὐτό

αὐτοί masc. nom. pl. αὐτός, αὐτή, αὐτό
αὐτόν masc. acc. sg. αὐτός, αὐτή, αὐτό
αὐτός masc. nom. sg. αὐτός, αὐτή, αὐτό
αὐτοῦ masc./neut. gen. sg. αὐτός, αὐτή, αὐτό
αὐτούς masc. acc. pl αὐτός, αὐτή, αὐτό
αὐτῷ masc. dat. sg. αὐτός, αὐτή, αὐτό
αὐτῶν masc./fem./neut. gen. pl. αὐτός, αὐτή, αὐτό
ἀφέωνται 3d pl. perf. ind. pass. ἀφίημι
ἀφῇ 3d sg. aor. subj. act. ἀφίημι

Β

βάλλει 3d sg. pres. ind. act. βάλλω
βαρεῖαι fem. nom. pl. βαρύς
βίον masc. acc. sg. βίος
βίου masc. gen. sg. βίος

Γ

γάρ conj. γάρ
γεγεννημένον perf. ptcp. pass. masc./neut.
   acc./nom. sg. γεννάω
γεγεννημένος perf. ptcp. pass. masc. nom. sg.
   γεννάω
γεγέννηται 3d sg. perf. ind. pass. γεννάω
γεγόνασιν 3d pl. perf. ind. act. γίνομαι
γεννηθείς aor. ptcp. pass. masc. nom. sg. γεννάω
γεννήσαντα aor. ptcp. act. masc. acc. sg. γεννάω
γινώσκει 3d sg. pres. ind. act. γινώσκω
γινώσκετε 2d pl. pres. ind./impv. act. γινώσκω
γινώσκομεν 1st pl. pres. ind. act. γινώσκω
γινώσκωμεν 1st pl. pres. subj. act. γινώσκω
γινώσκων pres. ptcp. act. masc. nom. sg. γινώσκω
γλώσσῃ fem. dat. sg. γλῶσσα
γνωσόμεθα 1st pl. fut. ind. mid. γινώσκω
γράφομεν 1st pl. pres. ind. act. γράφω
γράφω 1st sg. pres. ind. act. γράφω

Δ

δ' conj. δέ
δέ conj. δέ
δέδωκεν 3d sg. perf. ind. act. δίδωμι
δι' prep. διά
διά prep. διά
διάβολος masc. nom. sg. διάβολος
διαβόλου masc. gen. sg. διάβολος
διάνοιαν fem. acc. sg. διάνοια
διδάσκει 3d sg. pres. ind. act. διδάσκω
διδάσκῃ 3d sg. pres. subj. act. διδάσκω
δίκαια neut. nom./acc. pl. δίκαιος
δίκαιον masc./neut. acc./nom. sg. δίκαιος
δίκαιος masc. nom. sg. δίκαιος
δικαιοσύνην fem. acc. sg. δικαιοσύνη
δοκιμάζετε 2d pl. pres. ind. impv. act. δοκιμάζω

δύναται 3d sg. pres. ind. pass. δύναμαι
δώσει 3d sg. fut. ind. act. δίδωμι

Ε

ἐάν particle ἐάν
ἑαυτά neut. acc. pl. ἑαυτοῦ
ἑαυτόν masc. acc. sg. ἑαυτοῦ
ἑαυτούς masc. acc. pl. ἑαυτοῦ
ἑαυτῷ masc./neut. dat. sg. ἑαυτοῦ
ἔγνω 3d sg. aor. ind. act. γινώσκω
ἔγνωκα 1st sg. perf. ind. act. γινώσκω
ἐγνώκαμεν 1st pl. perf. ind. act. γινώσκω
ἐγνώκατε 2d pl. perf. ind. act. γινώσκω
ἔγνωκεν 3d sg. perf. ind. act. γινώσκω
ἔγραψα 1st sg. aor. ind. act. γράφω
ἐγώ nom. sg. ἐγώ
ἐδίδαξεν 3d sg. aor. ind. act. διδάσκω
ἔδωκεν 3d sg. aor. ind. act. δίδωμι
ἐθεασάμεθα 1st pl. aor. ind. mid. θεάομαι
ἔθηκεν 3d sg. aor. ind. act. τίθημι
εἰ particle εἰ
εἰδῆτε 2d pl. 2d perf. subj. act. οἶδα
εἰδώλων neut. gen. pl. εἴδωλον
εἶναι pres. inf. act. εἰμί
εἴπῃ 3d sg. 2d aor. subj. act. λέγω
εἴπωμεν 1st pl. 2d aor. subj. act. λέγω
εἰς prep. εἰς
εἰσίν 3d pl. pres. ind. act. εἰμί
εἴχετε 2d pl. impf. ind. act. ἔχω
ἐκ prep. ἐκ
ἐκείνης fem. gen. sg. ἐκεῖνος
ἐκεῖνος masc. nom. sg. ἐκεῖνος
ἐλάβετε 2d pl. 2d aor. ind. act. λαμβάνω
ἐληλυθότα 2d perf. ptcp. act. masc. acc. sg.
   ἔρχομαι
ἐλθών 2d aor. ptcp. act. masc. nom. sg. ἔρχομαι
ἐλπίδα fem. acc. sg. ἐλπίς
ἔμπροσθεν prep. ἔμπροσθεν
ἐν prep. ἐν
ἕν neut. acc. sg. εἷς, μία, ἕν
ἐντολαί fem. nom. pl. ἐντολή
ἐντολάς fem. acc. pl. ἐντολή
ἐντολή fem. nom. sg. ἐντολή
ἐντολήν fem. acc. sg. ἐντολή
ἐνώπιον prep. ἐνώπιον
ἐξ prep. ἐκ
ἐξεληλύθασιν 3d pl. 2d perf. ind. act. ἐξέρχομαι
ἐξῆλθαν 3d pl. 2d aor. ind. act. ἐξέρχομαι
ἔξω adv. ἔξω
ἐπ' prep. ἐπί
ἐπαγγελία fem. nom. sg. ἐπαγγελία
ἐπηγγείλατο 3d sg. aor. ind. mid. ἐπαγγέλλομαι
ἐπιθυμία fem. nom. sg. ἐπιθυμία

ἔργα neut. nom./acc. pl. ἔργον
ἔργῳ neut. dat. sg. ἔργον
ἔρχεται 3d sg. pres. ind. mid. ἔρχομαι
ἐρωτήσῃ 3d sg. aor. subj. act. ἐρωτάω
ἐσμέν 1st pl. pres. ind. act. εἰμί
ἐσόμεθα 1st pl. fut. ind. mid. εἰμί
ἐστε 2d pl. pres. ind. act. εἰμί
ἔστιν 3d sg. pres. ind. act. εἰμί
ἔσφαξεν 3d sg. aor. ind. act. σφάζω
ἐσχάτη fem. nom. sg. ἔσχατος
ἐτύφλωσεν 3d sg. aor. ind. act. τυφλόω
ἐφανερώθη 3d sg. aor. ind. pass. φανερόω
ἔχει 3d sg. pres. ind. act. ἔχω
ἔχετε 2d pl. pres. ind./impv. act. ἔχω
ἔχῃ 3d sg. pres. subj. act. ἔχω
ἔχητε 2d pl. pres. subj. act. ἔχω
ἔχομεν 1st pl. pres. ind. act. ἔχω
ἔχοντα pres. ptcp. act. masc. acc. sg. ἔχω
ἔχωμεν 1st pl. pres. subj. act. ἔχω
ἔχων pres. ptcp. act. masc. nom. sg. ἔχω
ἐψηλάφησαν 3d pl. aor. ind. act. ψηλαφάω
ἑωράκαμεν 1st pl. perf. ind. act. ὁράω
ἑώρακεν 3d sg. perf. ind. act. ὁράω
ἕως adv. ἕως

Z

ζήσωμεν 1st pl. aor. subj. act. ζάω
ζωή fem. nom. sg. ζωή
ζωήν fem. acc. sg. ζωή
ζωῆς fem. gen. sg. ζωή

H

ἤ adv. ἤ
ἡ fem. nom. sg. ὁ, ἡ, τό
ἠγαπήκαμεν 1st pl. perf. ind. act. ἀγαπάω
ἠγάπησεν 3d sg. aor. ind. act. ἀγαπάω
ἤδη adv. ἤδη
ᾖ 3d sg. pres. subj. act. εἰμί
ᾐτήκαμεν 1st pl. perf. ind. act. αἰτέω
ἥκει 3d sg. pres. ind. act. ἥκω
ἠκούσατε 2d pl. aor. ind. act. ἀκούω
ἡμαρτήκαμεν 1st pl. perf. ind. act. ἁμαρτάνω
ἡμᾶς acc. pl. ἡμεῖς
ἡμεῖς nom. pl. ἡμεῖς
ἡμέρα fem. dat. sg. ἡμέρα
ἡμετέρα fem. nom. sg. ἡμέτερος
ἡμετέρων fem. gen. pl. ἡμέτερος
ἡμῖν dat. pl. ἡμεῖς
ἡμῶν gen. pl. ἡμεῖς
ἦν 3d sg. impf. ind. act. εἰμί
ἥν fem. acc. sg. ὅς, ἥ, ὅ
ἦσαν 3d pl. impf. ind. act. εἰμί
ἥτις fem. nom. sg. ὅστις, ἥτις, ὅτι

Θ

θάνατον masc. acc. sg. θάνατος
θανάτου masc. gen. sg. θάνατος
θανάτῳ masc. dat. sg. θάνατος
θαυμάζετε 2d pl. pres. ind./impv. act. θαυμάζω
θεῖναι aor. inf. act. τίθημι
θέλημα neut. acc. sg. θέλημα
θεόν masc. sg. acc. θεός
θεός masc. nom. sg. θεός
θεοῦ masc. gen. sg. θεός
θεῷ masc. dat. sg. θεός
θεωρῇ 3d sg. pres. subj. act. θεωρέω

I

ἴδετε 2d pl. 2d aor. impv. act. ὁράω
ἴδῃ 3d sg. 2d aor. subj. act. ὁράω
Ἰησοῦ masc. gen./dat. sg. Ἰησοῦς
Ἰησοῦν masc. acc. sg. Ἰησοῦς
Ἰησοῦς masc. nom. sg. Ἰησοῦς
ἱλασμόν masc. acc. sg. ἱλασμός
ἱλασμός masc. nom. sg. ἱλασμός
ἵνα conj. ἵνα
ἰσχυροί masc. nom. pl. ἰσχυρός

K

καθαρίζει 3d sg. pres. ind. act. καθαρίζω
καθαρίσῃ 3d sg. aor. subj. act. καθαρίζω
καθώς adv. καθώς
καί conj. καί
Κάϊν masc. indecl Κάϊν
καινήν fem. acc. sg. καινός
καρδία fem. nom. sg. καρδία
καρδίαν fem. acc. sg. καρδία
καρδίας fem. gen. sg. καρδία
κατά prep. κατά
καταγινώσκῃ 3d sg. pres. subj. act. καταγινώσκω
κεῖται 3d sg. pres. ind. mid. κεῖμαι
κλείσῃ 3d sg. aor. subj. act. κλείω
κληθῶμεν 1st pl. aor. subj. pass. καλέω
κοινωνία fem. nom. sg. κοινωνία
κοινωνίαν fem. acc. sg. κοινωνία
κόλασιν fem. acc. sg. κόλασις
κόσμον masc. acc. sg. κόσμος
κόσμος masc. nom. sg. κόσμος
κόσμου masc. gen. sg. κόσμος
κοσμῳ masc. dat. sg. κόσμος
κρίσεως fem. gen. sg. κρίσις

Λ

λαλοῦσιν 3d pl. pres. ind. act. λαλέω
λαμβάνομεν 1st pl. pres. ind. act. λαμβάνω
λέγω 1st sg. pres. ind. act. λέγω

λέγων pres. ptcp. act. masc. nom. sg. λέγω
λόγον masc. acc. sg. λόγος
λόγος masc. nom. sg. λόγος
λόγου masc. gen. sg. λόγος
λόγῳ masc. dat. sg. λόγος
λύσῃ 3d sg. aor. subj. act. λύω

Μ

μαρτυρία fem. nom. sg. μαρτυρία
μαρτυρίαν fem. acc. sg. μαρτυρία
μαρτυροῦμεν 1st pl. pres. ind. act. μαρτυρέω
μαρτυροῦν pres. ptcp. act. neut. nom. sg. μαρτυρέω
μαρτυροῦντες pres. ptcp. act. masc. nom. pl.
 μαρτυρέω
μεθ᾽ prep. μετά
μείζων masc./fem. nom. sg. μείζων
μείνῃ 3d sg. aor. subj. act. μένω
μεμαρτύρηκεν 3d sg. perf. ind. act. μαρτυρέω
μεμενήκεισαν 3d pl. pluperf ind. act. μένω
μένει 3d sg. pres. ind. act. μένω
μένειν pres. inf. act. μένω
μένετε 2d pl. pres. ind./impv. act. μένω
μενεῖτε 2d pl. fut. ind. act. μένω
μενέτω 3d sg. pres. impv. act. μένω
μένομεν 1st pl. pres. ind. act. μένω
μένουσαν pres. ptcp. act. fem. acc. sg. μένω
μένων pres. ptcp. act. masc. nom. sg. μένω
μετ᾽ prep. μετά
μετά prep. μετά
μεταβεβήκαμεν 1st pl. perf. ind. act. μεταβαίνω
μή negative particle μή
μηδέ conj. μηδέ
μηδείς masc. nom. sg. μηδείς, μηδεμία, μηδέν
μισεῖ 3d sg. pres. ind. act. μισέω
μισῇ 3d sg. pres. subj. act. μισέω
μισῶν pres. ptcp. act. masc. nom. sg. μισέω
μοι dat. sg. ἐγώ
μονογενῆ masc. acc. sg. μονογενής
μόνον masc./neut. acc./nom. sg. μόνος
μου gen. sg. ἐγώ

Ν

νεανίσκοι masc. nom./voc. pl. νεανίσκος
νενικήκατε 2d pl. perf. ind. act. νικάω
νικᾷ 3d sg. pres. ind. act. νικάω
νίκη fem. nom. sg. νίκη
νικήσασα aor. ptcp. act. fem. nom. sg. νικάω
νικῶν pres. ptcp. act. masc. nom. sg. νικάω
νῦν adv. νῦν

Ο

ὅ neut. nom. sg. ὅς
ὁ masc. nom. sg. ὁ, ἡ, τό

ὅθεν adv. ὅθεν
οἱ masc. nom. pl. ὁ, ἡ, τό
οἴδαμεν 1st pl. 2d perf. ind. act. οἶδα
οἴδατε 2d pl. 2d perf. ind. act. οἶδα
οἶδεν 3d sg. 2d perf. ind. act. οἶδα
ὅλος masc. nom. sg. ὅλος
ὅλου masc./neut. gen. sg. ὅλος
ὅμοιοι masc. nom. pl. ὅμοιος
ὁμολογεῖ 3d sg. pres. ind. act. ὁμολογέω
ὁμολογήσῃ 3d sg. aor. subj. act. ὁμολογέω
ὁμολογῶμεν 1st pl. pres. subj. act. ὁμολογέω
ὁμολογῶν pres. ptcp. act. masc. nom. sg.
 ὁμολογέω
ὅν masc. acc. sg. ὅς, ἥ, ὅ
ὄνομα neut. nom./acc. sg. ὄνομα
ὀνόματι neut. dat. sg. ὄνομα
ὅς masc. nom. sg. ὅς, ἥ, ὅ
ὅταν conj. ὅταν
ὅτι conj. ὅτι
οὐ negative particle οὐ
οὗ masc./neut. gen. sg. ὅς, ἥ, ὅ
οὐδέ conj. οὐδέ
οὐδείς masc. nom. sg. οὐδείς, οὐδεμία, οὐδέν
οὐδεμία fem. nom. sg. οὐδείς, οὐδεμία, οὐδέν
οὐκ negative particle οὐ
οὔπω adv. οὔπω
οὗτος masc. nom. sg. οὗτος, αὕτη, τοῦτο
οὕτως adv. οὕτως
οὐχ negative particle οὐ
ὀφείλει 3d sg. pres. ind. act. ὀφείλω
ὀφείλομεν 1st pl. pres. ind. act. ὀφείλω
ὀφθαλμοῖς masc. dat. pl. ὀφθαλμός
ὀφθαλμούς masc. acc. pl. ὀφθαλμός
ὀφθαλμῶν masc. gen. pl. ὀφθαλμός
ὀψόμεθα 1st pl. fut. ind. mid. ὁράω

Π

παιδία neut. nom./voc./acc. pl. παιδίον
παλαιά fem. nom. sg. παλαιός
παλαιάν fem. acc. sg. παλαιός
πάλιν adv. πάλιν
πᾶν neut. nom./acc. sg. πᾶς
πάντα neut. nom./acc. pl. πᾶς
πάντες masc. nom. pl. πᾶς
παντί masc./neut. dat. sg. πᾶς
πάντων masc./neut. gen. pl. πᾶς
παράγεται 3d sg. pres. ind. pass. παράγω
παράκλητον masc. acc. sg. παράκλητος
παρουσίᾳ fem. dat. sg. παρουσία
παρρησία fem. nom. sg. παρρησία
παρρησίαν fem. acc. sg. παρρησία
πᾶς masc. nom. sg. πᾶς
πᾶσα fem. nom. sg. πᾶς

πάσης fem. gen. sg. πᾶς
πατέρα masc. acc. sg. πατήρ
πατέρες masc. nom./voc. pl. πατήρ
πατήρ masc. nom. sg. πατήρ
πατρί masc. dat. sg. πατήρ
πατρός masc. gen. sg. πατήρ
πείσομεν 1st pl. fut. ind. act. πειθώ
πεπιστεύκαμεν 1st pl. perf. ind. act. πιστεύω
πεπίστευκεν 3d sg. perf. ind. act. πιστεύω
πεπληρωμένη perf. ptcp. pass. fem. nom. sg. πληρόω
πεποίηκεν 3d sg. perf. ind. act. ποιέω
περί prep. περί
περιεπάτησεν 3d sg. aor. ind. act. περιπατέω
περιπατεῖ 3d sg. pres. ind. act. περιπατέω
περιπατεῖν pres. inf. act. περιπατέω
περιπατῶμεν 1st pl. pres. subj. act. περιπατέω
πιστεύετε 2d pl. pres. ind./impv. act. πιστεύω
πιστεύουσιν pres. ptcp. act. masc. dat. pl. πιστεύω
πιστεύσωμεν 1st pl. aor. subj. act. πιστεύω
πιστεύων pres. ptcp. act. masc. nom. sg. πιστεύω
πίστις fem. nom. sg. πίστις
πιστός masc. nom. sg. πιστός
πλανάτω 3d sg. pres. impv. act. πλανάω
πλάνης fem. gen. sg. πλάνη
πλανῶμεν 1st pl. pres. ind. act. πλανάω
πλανώντων pres. ptcp. act. masc. gen. pl. πλανάω
πνεῦμα neut. nom./acc. sg. πνεῦμα
πνεύματα neut. nom./acc. pl. πνεῦμα
πνεύματι neut. dat. sg. πνεῦμα
πνεύματος neut. gen. sg. πνεῦμα
ποιεῖ 3d sg. pres. ind. act. ποιέω
ποιοῦμεν 1st pl. pres. ind. act. ποιέω
ποιῶμεν 1st pl. pres. subj. act. ποιέω
ποιῶν pres. ptcp. act. masc. nom. sg. ποιέω
πολλοί masc. nom. pl. πολύς
πονηρά neut. nom./acc. pl. πονηρός
πονηρόν masc./neut. acc./nom. sg. πονηρός
πονηρός masc. nom. sg. πονηρός
πονηροῦ masc. gen. sg. πονηρός
πονηρῷ masc. dat. sg. πονηρός
ποταπήν fem. acc. sg. ποτοπός
ποῦ adv. ποῦ
πρός prep. πρός
πρῶτος masc. nom. sg. πρῶτος
πώποτε adv. πώποτε
πῶς adv. πῶς

Σ

σαρκί fem. dat. sg. σάρξ
σαρκός fem. gen. sg. σάρξ
σκάνδαλον neut. nom./acc. sg. σκάνδαλον
σκότει neut. dat. sg. σκότος
σκοτία fem. nom. sg. σκοτία

σκοτίᾳ fem. dat. sg. σκοτία
σπέρμα neut. nom./acc. sg. σπέρμα
σπλάγχνα neut. nom./acc. pl. σπλάγχνον
σχῶμεν 1st pl. 2d aor. subj. act. ἔχω
σωτῆρα masc. acc. sg. σωτήρ

Τ

τά neut. nom./acc. pl. ὁ, ἡ, τό
τάς fem. acc. pl. ὁ, ἡ, τό
ταῦτα neut. acc. pl. οὗτος, αὕτη, τοῦτο
ταύτην fem. acc. sg. οὗτος, αὕτη, τοῦτο
τεθεάμεθα 1st pl. perf. ind. mid. θεάομαι
τεθέαται 3d sg. perf. ind. mid. θεάομαι
τέκνα neut. nom./voc./acc. pl. τέκνον
τεκνία neut. nom./voc./acc. pl. τεκνίον
τελεία fem. sg. nom. τέλειος
τετελειωμένη perf. ptcp. pass. fem. nom. sg. τελειόω
τετελείωται 3d sg. perf. ind. pass. τελειόω
τῇ fem. dat. sg. ὁ, ἡ, τό
τήν fem. acc. sg. ὁ, ἡ, τό
τηρεῖ 3d sg. pres. ind. act. τηρέω
τηρῇ 3d sg. pres. subj. act. τηρέω
τηροῦμεν 1st pl. pres. ind. act. τηρέω
τηρῶμεν 1st pl. pres. subj. act. τηρέω
τηρῶν pres. ptcp. act. masc. nom. sg. τηρέω
τῆς fem. gen. sg. ὁ, ἡ, τό
τί neut. nom. sg. τίς
τι neut. nom./acc. sg. τις
τίνος masc./fem./neut. gen. sg. τίς
τίς masc./fem. nom. sg. τίς
τις masc./fem. nom. sg. τις
τό neut. nom./acc. sg. ὁ, ἡ, τό
τοῖς masc./neut. dat. pl. ὁ, ἡ, τό
τόν masc. acc. sg. ὁ, ἡ, τό
τοῦ masc./neut. gen. sg. ὁ, ἡ, τό
τούς masc. acc. pl. ὁ, ἡ, τό
τοῦτο neut. nom./acc. sg. οὗτος, αὕτη, τοῦτο
τούτου neut./masc. sg. gen. οὗτος, αὕτη, τοῦτο
τούτῳ neut./masc. dat. sg. οὗτος, αὕτη, τοῦτο
τρεῖς masc./fem. nom. pl. τρεῖς
τῷ masc./neut. dat. sg. ὁ, ἡ, τό
τῶν masc./fem./neut. gen. pl. ὁ, ἡ, τό

Υ

ὕδατι neut. dat. sg. ὕδωρ
ὕδατος neut. gen. sg. ὕδωρ
ὕδωρ neut. nom./acc. sg. ὕδωρ
υἱόν masc. acc. sg. υἱός
υἱός masc. sg. nom. υἱός
υἱοῦ masc. gen. sg. υἱός
υἱῷ masc. dat. sg. υἱός

ὑμᾶς acc. pl. ὑμεῖς
ὑμεῖς nom. pl. ὑμεῖς
ὑμῖν dat. pl. ὑμεῖς
ὑπάγει 3d sg. pres. ind. act. ὑπάγω
ὑπέρ prep. ὑπέρ

Φ

φαίνει 3d sg. pres. ind. act. φαίνω
φανερά neut. nom./acc. pl. φανερός
φανερωθῇ 3d sg. aor. subj. pass. φανερόω
φανερωθῶσιν 3d pl. aor. subj. pass. φανερόω
φόβον masc. acc. sg. φόβος
φόβος masc. nom. sg. φόβος
φοβούμενος pres. ptcp. pass. masc. nom. sg.
  φοβέομαι
φυλάξατε 2d pl. aor. impv. act. φυλάσσω
φῶς neut. nom./acc. sg. φῶς
φωτί neut. dat. sg. φῶς

Χ

χαρά fem. nom. sg. χαρά
χάριν prep. χάριν

χεῖρες fem. nom. pl. χείρ
χρείαν fem. acc. sg. χρεία
χρῖσμα neut. nom./acc. sg. χρῖσμα
Χριστόν masc. acc. sg. Χριστός
Χριστός masc. nom. sg. Χριστός
Χριστοῦ masc. gen. sg. Χριστός
Χριστῷ masc. dat. sg. Χριστός

Ψ

ψευδόμεθα 1st pl. pres. ind. mid./pass.
  ψεύδομαι
ψευδοπροφῆται masc. nom. pl. ψευδοπροφήτης
ψεῦδος neut. nom. sg. ψεῦδος
ψεύστην masc. acc. sg. ψεύστης
ψεύστης masc. nom. sg. ψεύστης
ψυχάς fem. acc. pl. ψυχή
ψυχήν fem. acc. sg. ψυχή

Ω

ὥρα fem. nom. sg. ὥρα
ὡς conj. ὡς

WORKS CITED

Biblical Texts

Aland, Barbara, Kurt Aland, Johannes Karavidopoulos, Carlo M. Martini, and Bruce Metzger, eds. *The Greek New Testament.* 4th rev. ed. Stuttgart: Deutsche Bibelgesellschaft and United Bible Societies, 1993.
———. *Novum Testamentum Graece.* 27th ed. Stuttgart: Deutsche Bibelgesellschaft, 1993.
Rahlfs, Alfred, ed. *Septuaginta.* Stuttgart: Deutsche Bibelgesellschaft, 1979.

Commentaries

Brown, Raymond E. *The Epistles of John.* Anchor Bible. Garden City, N.Y.: Doubleday, 1982.
Bultmann, Rudolf. *The Johannine Epistles.* Hermeneia. Philadelphia: Fortress, 1973.
Grayston, Kenneth. *The Johannine Epistles.* New Century Bible Commentary. Grand Rapids: Eerdmans, 1984.
Johnson, Thomas F. *1, 2, 3, John.* New International Biblical Commentary. Peabody, Mass.: Hendrickson, 1993.
Marshall, I. Howard. *The Epistles of John.* New International Commentary on the New Testament. Grand Rapids: Eerdmans, 1978.
Schnackenburg, Rudolf. *The Johannine Epistles: Introduction and Commentary.* Translated by Reginald and Ilse Fuller. New York: Crossroad, 1992.
Smalley, S. S. *1, 2, 3 John.* Word Biblical Commentary. Waco, Tex.: Word, 1984.
Stott, John R. W. *The Letters of John: An Introduction and Commentary.* Rev. ed. Tyndale New Testament Commentaries. Grand Rapids: Eerdmans, 1988.
Westcott, B. F. *The Epistles of St. John: The Greek Text with Notes and Essays.* London: Macmillan and Company, 1886; reprint Grand Rapids: Eerdmans, 1966.

Concordances

Hatch, Edwin, and H. A. Redpath. *A Concordance to the Septuagint and the Other Greek Versions of the Old Testament (Including the Apocryphal Books).* 3 vols. Oxford: Clarendon Press, 1897; reprint, Grand Rapids: Baker, 1998.
Kohlenberger, John R., III, Edward W. Goodrick, and James A. Swanson. *The Exhaustive Concordance to the Greek New Testament.* Grand Rapids: Zondervan, 1995.

Works on Exegetical Method

Carson, D. A. *Exegetical Fallacies*. 2d ed. Grand Rapids: Baker, 1996.
Fee, Gordon. *New Testament Exegesis*. Louisville: Westminster John Knox, 1993.

Grammars

Blass, F., and A. Debrunner. *A Greek Grammar of the New Testament*. Translated and edited by R. W. Funk. Chicago: University of Chicago Press, 1961.
Brooks, James A., and Carlton L. Winbery. *Syntax of New Testament Greek*. Lanham, Md.: University Press of America, 1979.
Burton, Ernest DeWitt. *Syntax of the Moods and Tenses in New Testament Greek*. 3d ed. Edinburgh: T. & T. Clark, 1898; reprint, Grand Rapids: Kregel, 1976.
Chamberlain, William Douglas. *An Exegetical Grammar of the Greek New Testament*. Grand Rapids: Baker, 1979.
Dana, H., and J. R. Mantey. *A Manual Grammar of the Greek New Testament*. New York: Macmillan, 1959.
Fanning, Buist M. *Verbal Aspect in New Testament Greek*. Oxford: Clarendon, 1990.
Goetchius, Eugene Van Ness. *The Language of the New Testament*. New York: Charles Scribner's Sons, 1965.
Greenlee, J. Harold. *A Concise Exegetical Grammar of New Testament Greek*. 5th ed. Grand Rapids: Eerdmans, 1986.
Hewett, James A. *New Testament Greek: A Beginning and Intermediate Grammar*. Peabody, Mass.: Hendrickson, 1986.
Machen, J. Gresham. *New Testament Greek for Beginners*. New York: Macmillan, 1951.
McKay, K. L. *A New Syntax of the Verb in New Testament Greek: An Aspectual Approach*. Studies in Biblical Greek 5. New York: Peter Lang, 1994.
Moule, C. F. D. *An Idiom Book of New Testament Greek*. 2d ed. Cambridge: Cambridge University Press, 1959.
Moulton, James Hope. *Prolegomena*. Vol. 1 of *A Grammar of New Testament Greek*. Edinburgh: T. & T. Clark, 1985.
Moulton, James Hope, and W. F. Howard, *Accidence and Word-Formation*. Vol. 2 of *A Grammar of New Testament Greek*, by J. H. Moulton. Edinburgh: T. & T. Clark, 1986.
Mounce, William D. *Basics of Biblical Greek*. Grand Rapids: Zondervan, 1993.
Porter, Stanley E. *Idioms of the Greek New Testament*. 2d ed. Sheffield: Sheffield Academic Press, 1996.
Robertson, A. T. *A Grammar of the Greek New Testament in the Light of Historical Research*. Nashville: Broadman, 1934.
Robertson, A. T., and W. Hersey Davis. *A New Short Grammar of the Greek New Testament*. New York: Harper, 1931; reprint, Grand Rapids: Baker, 1977.
Turner, Nigel. *Syntax*. Vol. 3 of *A Grammar of New Testament Greek*, by J. H. Moulton. Edinburgh: T. & T. Clark, 1963.

Turner, Nigel. *Style*. Vol. 4 of *A Grammar of New Testament Greek*, by J. H. Moulton. Edinburgh: T. & T. Clark, 1976.

Vaughan, Curtis, and Virtus E. Gideon. *A Greek Grammar of the New Testament: A Workbook Approach to Intermediate Grammar*. Nashville: Broadman, 1979.

Wallace, Daniel B. *Greek Grammar Beyond the Basics*. Grand Rapids: Zondervan, 1996.

Wenham, J. W. *The Elements of New Testament Greek*. Cambridge: Cambridge University Press, 1965; reprint, 1991.

Young, R. A. *Intermediate New Testament Greek: A Linguistic and Exegetical Approach*. Nashville: Broadman, 1994.

Zerwick, Maximilian. *Biblical Greek: Illustrated by Examples*. Translated by Joseph Smith. Rome: Pontifical Biblical Institute, 1963.

Historical and Cultural Backgrounds

Bromiley, Geoffrey W. *The International Standard Bible Encyclopedia*. 4 vols. Grand Rapids: Eerdmans, 1988.

Freedman, David Noel. *The Anchor Bible Dictionary*. 6 vols. New York: Doubleday, 1992.

Lexical and Grammatical Aids

Greenlee, J. Harold. *A New Testament Greek Morpheme Lexicon*. Grand Rapids: Baker, 1983.

Haas, C., M. DeJonge, and J. L. Swellengrebel. *A Translator's Handbook of the Letters of John*. London: United Bible Societies, 1972.

Kubo, Sakae. *A Reader's Greek-English Lexicon of the New Testament and a Beginner's Guide for the Translation of New Testament Greek*. Grand Rapids: Zondervan, 1975.

Metzger, Bruce M. *Lexical Aids for Students of New Testament Greek*. Princeton: Theological Book Agency, 1975.

Mounce, William D. *The Analytical Lexicon to the Greek New Testament*. Grand Rapids: Zondervan, 1993.

Robertson, A. T. *The General Epistles and The Revelation of John*. Vol. 6 of *Word Pictures in the New Testament*. Nashville: Broadman, 1933.

Rogers, Cleon, Jr., and Cleon Rogers III. *New Linguistic and Exegetical Key to the Greek New Testament*. Grand Rapids: Zondervan, 1998.

Smith, David. *The Epistles of John*. Vol. 5 of *The Expositor's Greek Testament*. Edited by W. R. Nicoll. London: Hodder & Stoughton, 1900; reprint, Grand Rapids: Eerdmans, 1970.

Vincent, Marvin R. *The Writings of John*. Vol. 2 of *Word Studies in the New Testament*. New York: Charles Scribner's Sons, 1887; reprint, Grand Rapids: Eerdmans, 1975.

Wuest, Kenneth. *The New Testament: An Expanded Translation.* Grand Rapids: Eerdmans, 1985.

Zerwick, Max, and Mary Grosvenor. *A Grammatical Analysis of the Greek New Testament.* 5th rev. ed. Rome: Biblical Institute Press, 1996.

Lexicons and Dictionaries

Balz, Horst, and Gerhard Schneider, eds. *Exegetical Dictionary of the New Testament.* 3 vols. Grand Rapids: Eerdmans, 1990–1993.

Bauer, Walter. *A Greek-English Lexicon of the New Testament and Other Early Christian Literature.* 2d ed. Translated by W. F. Arndt and F. W. Gingrich. Revised and edited by F. W. Danker. Chicago: University of Chicago Press, 1979.

Brown, Colin, ed. *The New International Dictionary of New Testament Theology.* 4 vols. Grand Rapids: Zondervan, 1975–1986.

Kittel, Gerhard, and Gerhard Friedrich, eds. *Theological Dictionary of the New Testament.* 10 vols. Translated by G. W. Bromiley. Grand Rapids: Eerdmans, 1964–1976.

Liddell, Henry G., and Robert Scott. *A Greek-English Lexicon.* 9th ed. Revised by H. S. Jones and Roderick McKenzie, with a revised supplement. Oxford: Clarendon Press, 1996.

Louw, Johannes P., and Eugene A. Nida. *Greek-English Lexicon of the New Testament Based on Semantic Domains.* 2 vols. New York: United Bible Societies, 1988–1989.

Moulton, James Hope, and George Milligan. *The Vocabulary of the Greek Testament.* London: Hodder & Stoughton, 1930; reprint, Peabody, Mass.: Hendrickson, 1997.

Spicq, Ceslas. *Theological Lexicon of the New Testament.* Translated and edited by James D. Ernest. 3 vols. Peabody, Mass.: Hendrickson, 1994.

Textual Criticism

Aland, Barbara, and Kurt Aland. *The Text of the New Testament.* 2d ed. Grand Rapids: Eerdmans, 1989.

Greenlee, Harold J. *Introduction to New Testament Textual Criticism.* Rev. ed. Peabody, Mass.: Hendrickson, 1995.

Metzger, Bruce M. *The Text of the New Testament: Its Transmission, Corruption, and Restoration.* 3d ed. New York: Oxford University Press, 1992.

———. *A Textual Commentary on the Greek New Testament.* 2d ed. Stuttgart: Deutsche Bibelgesellschaft, 1994.

Word Studies

Barclay, William. *New Testament Words.* Philadelphia: Westminster Press, 1974.

Trench, Richard Chenevix. *Synonyms of the New Testament.* Grand Rapids: Eerdmans, 1975.